THE TIME OF TH

Merry Xmas Mum
love from
Vic Jay

BY THE SAME AUTHOR

Twenty-two books for or about children
OGF, a novel
World War Two Wasn't All *Hell*, an autobiography
The Palace of Signs, an autobiography
Supernatural! *Australian Encounters*

THE TIME OF THEIR LIVES!

Remembering Yesterday's Australia

Keith Smith

ALLEN & UNWIN

First published in 1993

Allen & Unwin Pty Ltd
9 Atchison Street, St Leonards, NSW 2065 Australia

National Library of Australia
Cataloguing-in-Publication entry:

Smith, Keith, 1917–
The time of their lives.
ISBN 1 86373 469 4.
1. Aged—Australia—Interviews. 2. Australia
—Social conditions. 3. Australia—Social life
and customs. 4. Australia—History. I. Title.
994

Set in 11/12.5 Baskerville by Graphicraft Typesetters, Hong Kong

Printed by Chong Moh Offset Printing, Singapore

10 9 8 7 6 5 4 3 2 1

Foreword

It is refreshing to note that despite the increasing popularity of satellites, computers, fax and other electronic wonders, our most common form of communication is still the spoken word.

Synthetic speech cannot equal it, just as music reproduced 'perfectly' on a synthesizer cannot equal the warmth and romance of a Chopin waltz played by a gifted pianist.

Neither can a country's history, dredged up by latter-day historians and told third-hand, compare with the lively, perceptive reminiscences of elderly people who were a part of it, who helped to shape it, or while on the sidelines witnessed and remembered the drama of it.

In the late 1940s elderly men and women were a treasure-trove of information about Australia's early days. Yet at the time there was little interest in collecting and preserving this information. In 1948, while in Tasmania in search of historical material for a radio program, I visited the Hobart Museum where hundreds of photographs of convicts, the last of many transported in the 1860s, were on display. The pictures were daguerreotypes and their quality was so good that they might have been taken only a few days before. The exhibition was fascinating, yet the photographs were withdrawn from display soon afterwards and despite persistent enquiries I never discovered what happened to them.

Little wonder then that a few years later, in the early 1950s while talking with old people about life when they were young I saw the need to preserve their memories before it was too late. I devised a radio program devoted to their reminiscences which I called '—but Not Forgotten'.

The ABC liked it, broadcast it weekly and some interesting personalities emerged, among them country people who as children had played on the streets of Gulgong during the 1870s gold rush, a man who designed, built and flew an aeroplane in 1911 (only eight years after the Wright brothers flew theirs), some women who fought for equal opportunity in the professions one hundred years before similar demands from women began to bear fruit in the 1980s and 1990s, and many more.

I had to be patient when talking with them. I slowed my usual pace by half, resisted the temptation to jump in with questions and stopped recording when (as old people are apt to do) they began to ramble, then 'joined them on' to their previous comments so that when edited each spoke at some length alone—without interruptions from me.

My technique paid off. Encouraged by my interest they recalled a way of life long gone: colloquial Australian history spanning a period of one hundred years from the 1870s to the 1970s. Their memories, recorded first on wire, then acetate-coated discs and finally tape, provided a lucid and permanent record of life as it was in less-complex times.

If it's true that an important function of history-writing is to make one feel part of it, these reminiscences will serve the reader well. Elderly men and women talking about big events in their lives before and after the turn of the century, bring the past close to the present, while older readers will no doubt identify with a way of life they might have almost forgotten. Like artists putting the finishing touches to a painting, the old people added highlights to the social history of their times, illuminating a picture of Australian life which might otherwise have been overlooked without them.

Were the Australians of yesteryear very different from those of today? My first impression when hearing the tapes again and transcribing them recently is that they talked without much embellishment: talked less than we do today but seemed to say more. They were not taciturn but didn't feel obliged to qualify what they said with further explanation; probably they would have described their approach as 'sensible'.

Nobody appeared to question anything then. It was a time of master and man from the earliest period until well into the twentieth century; everybody knew his place and did as he—or she—was told. Not surprising that, as a result, horrific events like World War I, the death lists, the flu epidemic which followed and other disasters were accepted without question and none of those who told me about them appeared to have thought about them later with regret. Strange too that few if any looked back on their youthful years with much affection or called them 'the good old days'. Apparently there were few worth mentioning in Australia ninety or one hundred years ago.

The rigid class structure before and after 1900 might have had something to do with it. It showed itself in a variety of ways, some of them amusing, but by the 1930s the Depression—a great leveller—had reduced most Australians to a state of comparative poverty. However, life was not all bad. According to some who lived through the Depression, it did not make Australians more grasping and selfish as some analysts would have us believe, but drew people closer together and made them more considerate of each other than they had been in better times. I gained these impressions not always from what I was told but rather from the way it was said.

I had more trouble than I expected hunting for pictures to accompany the text. A surprise: photographs taken from the 1880s until the outbreak of war in 1914 were not hard to find; most were studio portraits taken in the days when such pictures were looked on as an important part of a family's history. Yet despite the popularity of the Box Brownie—and later, folding cameras—during the 1920s, 1930s and 1940s, few 'snaps' taken during those years seem to have survived and negatives were almost non-existent. Frequently, old people told me, 'I didn't have any pictures taken of me when I was young'.

Why was this oral history not published before? Because history need not be hurried and I was waiting for a time when I thought it would be best appreciated. I think that time is now. In a rapidly-changing Australia I sense public anxiety that our history seems to be slipping away from us, pushed aside by the excitement of change which is often mistaken for progress. It's time also to preserve our history before much of it disappears for good.

Nearly all of those who appear in these pages have passed on by now, but fortunately their memories remain and I thank them again for their contribution.

I fancy readers of *The Time of their Lives!* will want to do the same.

KEITH SMITH

Contents

Illustrations

Acknowledgements

The author wishes to thank the following—and others—who have given freely of their time and knowledge during the writing of *The Time of their Lives!*

Nancy Bird, Kylie Winkworth, Percy Campbell, Loftus Hyde, Sydney Levine, former members of the Tivoli ballet, Dawn Troy, Joe Scruse, Eileen Fitzer, G.U. and Barbara Allen, Frank Walters, Ernest Henry, Jack Hepher, Lily Leary, Douglas Ramsay, Gulgong Historical Society Inc. (Roma Wallis), The Mitchell Library, David Jones Ltd (Barbara Horton), The NSW Police Department (Caleb William), Taronga Park Zoo (Lyn Green), Ray Mitchell (journalist), The Salvation Army (Envoy George Hazel), Westpac (Lyn Milton), Australia Post (Ross McLaughlin), Rita Cornish, Virginia Ransom, Victor Richardson, Margaret Wood, Enid Gilbert, Allison Bennett, NSW Education Department (Jim Fletcher), Isabelle Hooper, Connie Bartley, Enid Jephcott, The Pharmaceutical Society of Australia (Ross Brown), Sam van der Sluice, Sadie Gale, Neville Singleton, NSW State Transit (David Keenan) Tempe Bus and Truck Museum (Dave Wilson), Ray Le Sueur, Hudson Shaw, NSW Conservatorium of Music (Claire McCoy), Mrs E. Myers.

Introduction

Great events in world history have been well documented but for most of us there is a greater fascination in learning about the life-styles of our ancestors who lived, loved and lingered for a time on the same patch we occupy today.

The Time of their Lives! then is not an official, dry-as-dust account of our past, but a lively record of life in city and country, most of it recalled by elderly Australians who were a part of it and recorded by them on tape in the 1950s and 1960s.

Their memories of events big and small, important and unimportant provide an interesting mosaic of past Australian life, illustrating how each generation leaves its mark on those which follow.

Gulgong gold

'There were about twenty-five saloons, lots of dance halls, billiard halls and pubs here in the seventies,' the old bloke told me. 'And the girls! I don't know where they all came from but they were beautiful! The miners loved 'em all. Once, a famous actress—Maggie Oliver was her name—came up here in a Cobb and Co. coach, the miners met it outside the town, took the horses out of the shafts and pulled it into town themselves! And if the miners liked women in the shows they would hop up on the stage and shove gold nuggets down the fronts of their dresses! What great times they were!'

Harry Adams, a blacksmith during his long working life, was ninety years old, his face as lined and gnarled as the wood in the three-rail fence we were sitting on, and he was talking about what life was like in Gulgong, New South Wales during the turbulent days of the great gold rush in the 1870s.

'There were 25 000 miners here then living in calico tents or wooden slab huts with stringy-bark roofs . . . all after the gold, and only three police to keep them in order. There *was* a bit of fighting in the streets and arguments over mining licences but that was about it. All they wanted was the yellow stuff and they would put up with any hardship to get it.

'In the ten years of the rush they took out 483 000 ounces of gold, and they reckoned that just as much was sold illegally. Think of it . . . thirty-three square miles of tents and huts and claims—' He shook his head as though even he found it hard to believe so long afterwards.

Harry was my first contact when I visited Gulgong, 304 kilometres northwest of Sydney in the early 1950s to record a radio documentary. Already I'd noticed that it was a town where the past seemed reluctant to yield to the present because so much of the past remained, from the weatherworn mullock heaps standing like silent sentinels around its outskirts to the old banks, pubs and other buildings in its higgledy-piggledy Mayne Street, macadamised now but following the same muddy tracks which had been its main drag eighty years before, and where Harry had played as a boy.

He talked on and it wasn't hard to imagine the rows of calico tents, the slab huts, the bullock teams, the frantic excitement when a strike was made and the revelry in the pubs and dance halls. Harry's recollections of how the needy and the greedy descended in their thousands on Gulgong were spellbinding enough, but what hit me with a wallop was the fact that I was listening, not to somebody spouting Australian history from a textbook or retelling stories third- or fourth-hand, but that old Harry Adams was actually there when it happened!

Nothing could come closer to Australian history than that, and it set the standard for many other interviews I recorded with Australian old-timers back in the 1950s. Their unique memories for the most part would be lost unless they were recorded by a nosy reporter like myself and held until a later day when they would be considered valuable.

There seemed no end to the number of elderly 'historians' in Gulgong, all ready with a word or two about their youth in the 'hub of the world' as the miners liked to call it then.

An elderly lady described how the rush began in 1870: 'A man my family knew named Tom Saunders was tending sheep on a property at Red Hill. It was after a heavy shower of rain and he saw something shining in the grass. He got off his horse and had a look. It was a nugget of bright gold. He had a pick with him and he started fossicking. In two hours he picked up nuggets weighing fourteen ounces!

'He was so excited he rode over to Two Mile Flat and showed his find to Sergeant O'Donnel the policeman there. The news spread like wildfire and within two weeks, five hundred miners arrived and had shafts sunk around the town. Then thousands more came in drays and carts or on foot and horseback carrying dishes, cradles, picks and shovels and all their worldly possessions.

'The names of some of the claims and syndicates were very romantic,' she remembered: 'Black Swan, All Nations, Great Western, Wait-A-While, Moonlight and so many more. Some miners became rich overnight. I remember that with only shallow sinkings there were finds of up to fourteen and fifteen ounces, sometimes in a single load and that wasn't counting the nuggets!

Citizens on the street in Gulgong during the 1870s (Holtermann collection)

'But for every successful shaft there were many more that were duffers. Still, the feeling that luck might be just around the corner drove everybody on.'

Another elderly 'historian' said, 'I'm eighty-eight and I've been prospecting around here all my life. I've had good and bad patches. The biggest nugget I found weighed a good eight ounces, but nobody took much notice of that in those days; there were bigger ones being found all the time. A mate found a 32-ounce nugget, and once my father found one weighing 42 ounces out the back of where I live today, only a quarter of a mile from Gulgong.'

'Far down?' I asked.

'About four feet six. I still go prospecting there and often pick up a pennyweight or two.'

'With your father's luck and with the money he got for his 42-ounce nugget . . . what did he do with it? . . . save it?'

He looked at me as though I wasn't all there. 'Nah . . . he spent it on prospecting. Whenever you made anything you always spent it looking for more.'

On a more modest note another old chap reported, 'In those days when we were young you could earn six or seven bob a week from fossicking. I know because I did it! But I'd never earn more than fifteen bob going around cradling. There were four in my family and I had to help keep the lot with that. But it weren't too bad. Meat was only a penny halfpenny a pound.'

'The best steak was threepence a pound,' another white-haired prospector in his eighties remembered. 'Blucher boots were four-and-six a pair, a pair of moleskin pants the same, caps and flannel shirts were about two bob and bowler hats weren't much more.'

An old lady said, 'Beer and rum were the most popular drinks on the goldfields in the 1870s and it was quite usual for miners to front up to the bars and pull out little bags from their pockets and take out nuggets to pay for drinks. Women wouldn't go into some of the pubs . . . it wasn't considered proper, but they were all lively places with chorus girls and music and singsongs and dancing. There were three theatres too and the best actors and actresses came up from Sydney to do plays in them. And of course there was the Opera House.'

'At nights the streets were noisy and always packed with people,' somebody else said, 'and lots of shops: blacksmiths for shoeing horses and forging and sharpening miners' tools, general stores, livery stables, drapers, banks, barbers and Chinese vegetable shops where you could buy enough vegetables for a week for a few pence. There were lots of families here, of course, and in 1870 they built a big slab and stringy-bark church and a hospital a year later.'

One old chap spoke slowly and was sure of his facts: 'I remember a man named John Skully. He was a baker in Gulgong. If miners were hard up and couldn't pay for bread—it was a penny halfpenny a loaf—Skully would take what was known as a sleeping share in their mines instead. He became a rich man from doing that, but in the end he spent the lot—'

Apparently, it was a case of easy come, easy go then, with the chance of a big strike always round the corner, and not only once. He went on, 'I knew another feller named Aldridge who sank a shaft down here where the railway is and struck it rich first time. He got so much gold out of it and made so much money he ended up with three wives and seven or eight racehorses. Then he duffered out and lost the lot, so he went over to Lambing Flat (now called Young) and struck it rich there, too. He went through that lot too,' the old man laughed, 'then it was back to Gulgong and he sank another shaft up near the hospital and the same thing happened again. He died a pauper.'

Gulgong miners stop work for a photograph (Gulgong Museum)

'At one time Aldridge shoed some of his horses with gold horseshoes,' Harry Adams recalled calmly as though it was an everyday event. 'A lot of people will laugh if you tell them that, but it's a fact. My brother was a blacksmith like me and I saw him do it!'

One pointed to Loneragan's General Store on Mayne Street. 'That was built on gold. When they dug dirt out to put in the foundations they found enough to pay for the building.'

An old woman's eyes lit up as she recalled the excitement when there was a big strike: 'First, the red flag would go up—they always hoisted a red flag when it was really big—everybody would rush over, yelling and congratulating the finders and wanting to see the size of the nugget. Then the police would come to protect the shaft against thieves . . . there were a lot of crooks about. But the miners often protected themselves with man traps. They were like big rabbit traps that they set around the workings. They were really bear traps which had been brought over from Canada. And outside Gulgong, there were always the bushrangers, of course—'

'I remember when two of them were caught,' an old resident said. 'Thurston and Angel were their names. They were ambushed by police in Stewart's shop at a settlement called Belinfante seven miles out. They tried to hold up Stewart, but the police were waiting for them and shot them both. Stewart got shot, too. Both bushrangers were brought back to Gulgong; Angel was dead and they took him up to the hospital but Thurston was still alive and they laid him on the barroom floor of the Belmore Hotel. He died there.

The body of Thurston, the bushranger, was laid out in the bar of the Belmore Hotel

'People filed past afterwards to see the body. I was one of them. I was fourteen at the time. I still remember how he looked in death.'

I do, too. Somebody was thoughtful enough to take plaster death masks of both bushrangers and I saw them in the Gulgong Museum, along with thousands of other carelessly-arranged bits and pieces of Gulgong's memorable past: clothes, trinkets, children's toys, crockery, two Cobb and Co.'s coaches, phaetons, buggies, jinkers, spring carts, even goat carts. An interesting item was a doctor's journal which listed the various complaints which plagued the hard-working miners and revealed details of an epidemic which swept through Gulgong and laid the population low for a time.

It said nothing of course about the most common disease of all for which there was no cure: gold fever—which affected every man, woman and child in the town. It continued to rage until most of the 'easy' or surface gold had been won and bigger and more laborious methods were needed to search for the precious metal at greater depths, often requiring drilling through solid rock.

Gulgong's gold rush began to decline in 1875 when 'only' 6488 ounces of gold were won compared with 134 455 ounces six or seven years earlier; and new fields opening up at Temora and Parkes, together with an outbreak of typhoid hastened the exodus from Gulgong. By 1880 its great days were over.

I wanted to question the old people about that, about Henry Lawson too who was born and raised here, about Merlin the photographer who photographed every store, school and many aspects of life in Gulgong during the gold rush, but they showed little interest until I mentioned gold again and they sparked up. One could say it was the currency of their conversation and who could blame them for wanting to dwell on what had been the most exciting time of their lives during such a dramatic period in Australia's history? I asked if any of them knew where gold could be found now, in the 1950s, more than eighty years later.

One shook his head. 'Plenty left,' he said, 'but it's all too deep. Another: 'If I had the money to set up a plant at Adam's Lead I'd do good. There was plenty left behind after the rush.'

Others were less optimistic: 'No good now' or 'Even if you had a cradle or a banjo, you couldn't make a living out of it'. 'And you'd need help,' another said. 'Get a man to swing a shovel for you today and he would work himself out of it before he was four feet down.'

Another agreed. 'When I was a boy and the rush was on there was much work going on with whip poles and windlasses and there were big finds, but all you can do today is fossick. I knocked off doing it twelve months ago when I was eighty-five. I couldn't get anybody to help me work the old way. Young fellers won't take it on—'

'I often go specking . . . lots of us do,' an old lady said, quite excited.

I asked what specking was. 'You do it after rain. You'll see people walking along the street with their hands behind their backs and their heads down, looking for specks washed down the gutters. I was working in my garden one day and I dug up a little nugget. It weighed a pennyweight.'

Altogether, the folks of Gulgong had given me a crystal-clear picture of Gulgong when they were young. I had shared the noisy goings-on in the pubs and saloons with the bewhiskered miners in their blucher boots, moleskin pants and flannel shirts, the excitement when some lucky bugger made a big strike . . . and all of it eighty years before when gold was king.

The tourist buses with their rubber neckers have long since rubbed the sharp edge off the town's history, and old Harry Adams and his kind have gone on to heavens unknown, and for no particular reason I am reminded of an old Baptist hymn of their time which begins 'In that beautiful land on that far away strand—' and finishes, '—on the streets of purest gold, where the sun it doth never go down.'

I'm sure that Harry and the others would have marvelled at 'a sun that never went down' but as for 'the streets of purest gold' they would have remained unimpressed. It would be all old hat to them.

A country childhood

Life in the country was always more gentle than in the cities, and when Australian pioneers talk about their beginnings in the backblocks they display a warmth and affection which is surprising bearing in mind the primitive conditions under which many of them lived.

One of them was Madeline Kempster. Born of Irish-Catholic parents in 1898 and one of a very large family, she was christened 'Madeline' she told me because her parents had run out of good Irish names and didn't know what else to call her.

Her recollections of a childhood spent in the Australian bush around the turn of the century are told in a series of sharp word pictures, and the only thing missing from this narrative is the depth of feeling she displayed when she recounted them:

'I was one of fourteen children born in a lovely, but isolated farming area at the top of the New England Ranges, about twelve miles from Ben Lomond and twenty-two from Glen Innes, near the headwaters of the McIntyre River. We loved that little stream.

I remember the winter nights . . . the family gathering around the wood fire in our home. There were two buildings: the house and the kitchen. It was usual then to build a house in two parts so that if a kitchen caught alight—and it happened sometimes—the rest of the house would be saved.

Both buildings were roofed with bark. That too was common in the 1890s and later. I can still see the big fire and hear it, too, because

Madeline Kempster

there was always a fountain suspended over it. All older Australians will know what a fountain is: a huge, black cast-iron kettle hanging from a blackened crook over the fire and with a tap that was always dripping; it had a little tin underneath to catch the drips.

I can still smell our kitchen and see it, too. There were no boards on the floor . . . just dirt trampled hard by many feet. In wet weather, a damp earthy smell would rise and mingle with that of the bark rotting on the roof. The walls were rough-wood slabs, and of course they shrank in time and the wind whistled through.

My father built that kitchen and the house alongside it. And wasn't he the wild Irishman! Tall and ruddy, I believe, but I only remember him with a long grey beard and twinkling eyes. He was the only one, I was told, who could manage me, because I was the most stubborn of all the children.

He built up the farm himself and grew potatoes and had some sheep which he knew by name, most of them . . . . I do remember that, but the farm didn't pay. It was too far from the markets so when my brothers were old enough and strong enough they went off shearing in order to send money home to Mother, because Father died when I was quite young. As a matter of fact, I saw him die.

My older brother, John, took over. He was a strange, quiet man but with a great love for us all. Of course, during those years all of us children took Mother for granted but now, looking back I realise all the hardships she must have lived through, yet not once as I remember did she complain.

With fourteen children in the family—nine girls and five boys—you may wonder how we were all clothed. My mother made everything we wore and as we grew up, us girls were able to help. I can still see Mum, bent over her old Singer sewing machine. And the younger children, of course wore only hand-me-downs.

No electricity then. We had one lamp which Dad had bought, and some of us made small lamps of our own to light our way to bed. These were bottles filled with kerosene and the rest made from a pen holder, a cut-down cotton reel and a length of wick we bought from a store in Ben Lomond.

The big event in our lives as children was the occasional trip to Ben Lomond . . . in the early years in a spring cart and later in a sulky. (What a day it was when we got the sulky!) We could hardly sleep the night before the trip which was always after we got a cheque from "the boys", as Mother called them, when they had been paid for shearing somewhere. We would get dressed up in our Sunday best and then the journey of twelve miles over a rough bush track with great ruts in it and with our tired old horse Anchor in front.

When we arrived in Ben Lomond there wasn't much to see: just two shops and some scattered houses but best of all, a railway station! Out in the bush we could hear only the distant rumbling of trains, but to see a train arriving and departing was really an event.

Shopping? We stocked up for a month at Mr Roxbury's general store. Each of us kids had been given a penny to spend and we squandered it on conversation lollies and bullseyes and ate them all the way home.

Mr Roxbury always gave us humbugs too, rolled up in a little bag. I can still see him doing it and how we watched to make sure he put them in with the groceries.

All of us walked to school, two miles there and two miles back. Fifteen other children attended and I don't remember learning much because our teacher was obviously a misfit. Oscar Cecil Belgrave Walker was his name. We all knew that because his initials were on all the books he owned, possibly because he thought we would steal them. He boarded at a farm nearby and one of my most vivid memories is that of reading the same lesson over and over again until we all knew it by heart.

Do you remember Pretty Dick? I do. He was a literary hero during the last century. Marcus Clarke wrote the story. It told of Pretty Dick, a lost child, the seven-year-old son of Richard Fielding, a shepherd—

"He was the merriest little fellow with eyes like pools of clear water, as violet as the skies at sunset, and his skin as white as milk under his little blue and white shirt." That is just a sample and I never thought much about how the story was written or how real it was because in those days we just stood up in class and read. Nobody explained anything or asked us any questions and when a child got tired, he or she sat down, the next one stood up and read and so on.

So honest was my mother that she couldn't stand this state of affairs at the school any longer. We were being taught nothing and she told the teacher, Oscar Cecil Belgrave Walker that she would have him removed.

Surprisingly, he said, "I don't blame you, Mrs Meehan . . . I don't blame you, at all—" And that is what she did. He was replaced by another teacher, Richard Currie, who taught us all that the other hadn't.

When I was twelve and my youngest brother, Frank was eight, Mother decided to sell out and move to Armidale in order to get me a high school education, so that, eventually, she said, I could go on to teachers college.

I graduated as a teacher in 1916. Years afterwards when I was married I went to live in Armidale and foolishly I visited my old home, but of course it was not the same and I shouldn't have gone back.'

Madeline Kempster (nee Meehan), a confirmed Catholic, abandoned her beliefs in later life and became an outspoken communist, a courageous move since communism was frowned on at the time. A particularly strongminded woman to the end, she died in 1979 aged eighty-one.

Saddlery and a smith

One day in the 1950s I went looking for the oldest harness maker in Australia and found two in a dimly-lit loft in a lane off Pitt Street, Sydney.

I nearly stumbled over the first. He was sitting in the middle of a great heap of straw. I asked him what he was doing.

'Looking for long stems,' he said, simply.

'Why?'

'Because I'm stuffin' horse collars!' he said in a tone which suggested that only an idiot would ask such a question, and went on to say, 'I'm seventy-three. I've been working at making and stuffing horse collars in the saddlery trade ever since 1902. When I started you could buy a good horse collar for four shillings. Today it'd cost you seven pounds. I reckon I'm the last horse-collar maker left in Australia.'

I was going to ask him his name but already he had gone back to looking for long stems so I moved on to a room at the other end of the loft, exchanging the sweet smell of fresh straw for that of neat's-foot oil and leather, and the taciturn horse-collar maker for a very old man with needle and thread in hand whom I found seated on a low stool surrounded by saddles.

It was James P. Talty. Nobody I had spoken to was sure of his age—opinions varied between ninety-one and one hundred years—but there were few workers in the dwindling horse-harness trade who hadn't worked with him or could remember a time when Talty hadn't been around, making saddles and harnesses for horses. He looked frail sitting there but his hand was firm as he plied the needle.

Mr J.P. Talty

I watched him for a moment or two before I introduced myself and then, with some cajoling he recalled Sydney's past before and after the turn of the century.

'I started in the trade in 1890. I think I was about fourteen. The wages were 2/6 a week and no pay for holidays but they gave us something for Christmas Day. There was nothing but horses to get about with when I started work. The buses in Sydney were pulled by horses. They ran up Crown Street to Oxford Street and out to Bondi.

In those days—1890s—there was something you would never see now: all the horses wore bonnets. And business was good then; we were making saddles for horses used in the Boer War. When my apprenticeship was over I went to work with the original firm of John Brush, the largest saddlery business in Australia at the time. It was a big trade then. One firm had thirty men making collars alone to go on horses.

The principal place for selling horses was Inglis's Bazaar which ran from Pitt Street to Castlereagh Street, and for heavier horses they had what was known as a "Ton Trial" up Brickfield Hill. They had a dray loaded with a ton of bricks, a horse was put in the dray and he had to drag it up the hill past Anthony Hordern's.

The average price then for a good draughthorse or saddle-horse was ten to twelve pounds. There were five or six different types of horses used in Sydney in the 1890s, ranging from ponies to light horses used in bakers' carts, then the heavier horses used in brick-carting and horses bred especially for carriage work.

On race days in Sydney there were special drags to carry the customers and they drove out along the Randwick Road past the toll bar that was there at the time between Kensington Road and Randwick. The driver would throw the money on the ground for the collector to pick up. Everybody had to pay the toll; it was part of the road tax.

Horses were highly thought of then. There was a man who said he could ride a horse from Bathurst to Sydney in one day and when he finished the course in Sydney, the horse dropped dead.

The fashionable carriages at that time were called Victorias. They had a coachman and a footman and two seats, one in the front and one at the back, and a place for another. There were a number of them around Sydney and their owners lived mostly at Darling Point and Double Bay.

I was twenty years old when the first cars came along and they were that crude, people didn't think much of them. In fact, one of the leading bookmakers in Sydney brought one out from France, and when he had to go into the city he used to go down William Street all right but when he came back the car couldn't pull up the hill and he had to go round the back way to Oxford Street so he could get home.

The roads at that time were very bad . . . all right for horses but no good for cars . . . especially over the mountains. Many a time, the owner of a car couldn't go up the hills and he had to turn the car and go up backwards, slowly.

No wonder it took many years for the motor car to become a menace to the horse.

Today, in 1956 there are 10 000 registered trotting horses in New South Wales. They still need horses—farmers and such people. What can you do up there in the bush without a man, a horse, a whip and a dog to get the cattle out of difficult places? And I say, for a thousand years if the mountains are here, and the cattle are here, they'll still need horses and whips and dogs!'

Like Mr Talty, Joseph Ryan was interested in horses and when I met him in 1960, he was one day short of his hundredth birthday. His impressions of Sydney when he disembarked from a sailing ship in the latter part of the last century were sharper than any history book could provide and his accent was still unmistakably Irish:

'The date I arrived can easily be calculated because I was twenty-four when I arrived, which makes the date of my arrival 1884. I landed at the worst time. Sydney was very dark, very sad and it was hard to get employment. I was a blacksmith and horseshoer. I found it hard to find work and I got only one day some weeks . . . sometimes none, but it was a good week when I got four days.

The wage for a blacksmith then was ten shillings a day, and a working day was eight and three-quarter hours.

In the 1890s, I remember food and lodgings were expensive . . . it cost eighteen shillings for a week's board, you had to pay threepence for a pint of beer, and a bottle of John Dewar's whisky cost four shillings.

Pleasures? Well, I liked going to the races and watching boxing which was very popular then . . . all bare-knuckle boxing. I didn't entertain the idea of becoming a companion to young ladies, although I admit two heads *is* better than one!

There is no comparison between life then and now [1960]. There has been such remarkable progress and prosperity. No need now for great effort . . . the workers today do a few days a week and most of them sit while they're doin' it!'

A cooper and a smeller

The great Australian thirst for beer has been constant since the earliest days of the colony, but not always the quality of the product.

'Snipers', 'Tanglefoot', 'Sheepwash' and 'Shypoo' were only some of the derogatory names given to early Australian beer. It was often sour with some brews renowned more as a laxative than welcome refreshment. The first commercial beer in Australia was brewed from Cape gooseberries and maize by John Boston in 1796, and what with hot weather and horse-drawn transport, beer and drinkers suffered accordingly. Also, some early publicans watered their beer and during the last century a Liquor Act, proclaimed in New South Wales outlawed the spiking of beer with fish poison, tobacco juice and opium!

Somehow though beer survived, and before it found a temporary resting place in the bottomless gut of thirsty Australians, it had to be kept in something, hence the age-old trade of cooperage or barrel making. I met Mr Datsun, a cooper, in the late 1950s and I was lucky because coopering was a vanishing trade; stainless steel beer casks were just around the corner . . .

'I started as an apprentice cooper in 1912. Wages then were about £2 10s a week. Barrels were made from oak: two kinds, English oak and American oak. They were used to carry beer, spirits and wine. It took me five years to learn the trade and be a qualified cooper.

It takes about three hours to make an eighteen-gallon beer cask. In my day all barrels and casks were bound with steel hoops. They lasted indefinitely when coopers made them. In the old days staves

Coopers at work in Tooth's Sydney brewery, c. early 1920s

were hand-dressed, jointed and hollowed and put into place and shaped by steam or fire. Leaks were few, if any. Reeds found in swamps were used in toe joints after being dried ("flags", they were called).

The cooper's trade is said to be one of the four oldest in the world, after carpentry, masonry and pottery. When I was a boy, around the turn of the century, little barrels were made to hold cheese, and others were used to carry nails—up to fifty pounds in weight. They were also used for storing fish, and coopers were employed on sailing ships, the old whalers, for that purpose. And salt beef for sailors was stored in wooden kegs.

Coopers always blockmarked the barrels they made with their initials or other identification marks. I was fifty years in the trade and I bet some of my barrels are still around somewhere.'

Later, still interested in beer, I was shown over a brewery and introduced to a Cockney who followed a trade I had never heard of. He said he was a barrel smeller.

Q. *Are you the only smeller in the brewery?*
A. Oh no . . . there are half a dozen what you'd call smellers.

Q. *Who smells best . . . are you the top one?*
A. Oh no. I can't say I'm the top one . . . all are about the same. If

one smeller has doubts he asks another to smell and say what he thinks of a barrel.

Q. *You all smell together then?*
A. That's right. If one has a cold he gets help from somebody else. I've been smelling, myself, for the past eight years.

Q. *How did you start?*
A. Well, I've been among casks for the past fifty years.

Q. *You've been smelling a long time.*
A. Yes. Very good. That's right.

Q. *Why do you smell a cask?*
A. To see if it's fit for beer. I smell between four and five hundred a day.

Q. *Are there many different smells in each cask?*
A. Oh yes . . . three or four. A slightly-off one is called musty . . . one that smells sharp is called sour, another is foul and finally, one unfit for beer is called a stinker.

Q. *That one must be from the bottom of the barrel?*
A. Yes.

Q. *I'd like to sniff a cask myself.*
A. There's a barrel here . . . just come in empty from a pub. Have a sniff and tell me what you think.

Q. (I sniff) *That's easy. It's sour.*
A. (He is contemptuous) Nahhh! You're wrong. That's a stinker!

Coopers—barrel makers—have disappeared altogether over the past thirty or forty years. They are not listed in the yellow pages. And barrel smellers? I didn't even bother looking them up.

Singleton's travels

From the 1890s until his death in 1971, Cyril Singleton, a railways engineer and amateur historian was an authority on Australian transport. His knowledge wasn't theoretical; there was little that had wheels or hoofs that hadn't carried him from one part of the country to another. Perhaps his impressions will stifle some of the complaints of present-day commuters who whinge when their air-conditioned inter-city buses arrive a few minutes late.

'I remember the old horse buses in Sydney. They travelled regularly from the Glebe to Circular Quay, connecting with boats for Parramatta. The inside of a horse bus was not worth writing home about; patrons sat facing each other, in wet weather the floor was covered with straw, and fares were handed up to the driver in charge of the horses through a small hole. You had to ring a bell to attract his attention and you dropped the pennies in his hand. There were no tickets.

When you wanted to get off you pushed open the back door which had a strap attached. The other end was tied to the driver's leg up at the front. The movement of the door pulled his leg and he stopped the bus. About that time somebody had the bright idea that more passengers could be carried if seats were put up on the roof in the open, and a vertical ladder was installed for climbing up there. The seats faced outwards and the men liked it; in good weather at least, they could smoke as much as they liked without being pestered by women who had to ride downstairs. Horse buses ran in Sydney from 1848 until 1914.

Cyril Singleton

Just after I got engaged I travelled in a Cobb and Co. coach to the Allen River near Gresford on the New South Wales north coast. It was a very wet day and there were a lot of calf hides on the roof, and what with the blood and brine dripping through it was not a very comfortable trip. The coach was hung on leather acting as springs and they weren't much use. The road was rough and by the time I reached Gresford I was very sore and knocked about.

On the upper Patterson River in that part of the world, one of the local cockies I knew owned a South African sulky and I rode in it with him sometimes. It had a single pole and two horses, and he needed it for crossing the river. There were sixteen crossings in the same number of miles and on one of them we had to stand up on the seats while the horses swam to the other side.

I recall the opening of the railway between Casino and South Brisbane. A train ferry called *Swallow* was used to carry the brake van and carriages across, while passengers had to use a steam ferry.

At the opening ceremony at Kyogle, the railways commissioner of the day, Mr Cleary, gave a speech. He was a great talker. He was standing on the front of the engine surrounded by local celebrities and other townspeople and talked on and on.

The Queensland commissioner of railways got very agitated, because Cleary's long-winded speech meant that the opening ceremonies at the other end, in Brisbane, would be delayed, so he went to the district superintendent and asked if there was any way he could stop the man from talking.

The superintendent rose to the occasion by getting up on the engine and blowing a long blast on the whistle. The eruption of people from around the front of the engine was wonderful to see! The New South Wales commissioner was most annoyed and looked for the driver and fireman but they were underneath the engine hammering away like blazes!

I was just seventeen years old when they built Sydney Central Railway Station. The site was that of the old Devonshire Street cemetery and to satisfy public sensitivity, bodies buried there had to be shifted. So they were dug up and conveyed on flat trucks to Bunnerong Cemetery which was near the site of the present powerhouse.

The workers were very casual about it all. There were tales that the bones got mixed up, with two right arms and two left legs in some coffins.

About trams: Melbourne was famous for its cable trams which ran between city and suburbs from 1885 until 1940. Each had a passenger car at the back and a dummy in front where the driver stood. Using a system of ratchets and gears he hooked the tram on to an underground cable and away it went. He simply released it and braked when he wanted to stop. There was an additional brake on the car behind, which the conductor wound up or down by hand on particularly steep hills. Cable trams were safe and reliable but people on pushbikes had to be careful on roads where the trams operated. Their wheels were much the same width as the grooves in the rails which were flush with the road and cyclists could be thrown if they got caught up in them.

Cable trams were introduced into Sydney in 1884 and ran until 1905.

The first steam trams were put into service in Sydney in 1879. They were curious-looking vehicles and consisted of two or three double-decker passenger cars on rails and hauled by small steam engines. The top decks had corridors with "toast rack" cars underneath. The latter were the first of many "toast rack" trams which became almost a permanent fixture in Sydney. Many present-day commuters will remember travelling in them on wet winter nights when the conductors, in dripping wet oilskins swung like monkeys along the outside of the trams collecting fares from each draughty compartment. The last of them, on the city-to-Bondi run were phased out in 1960.

Electric "toast rack" trams were first introduced into Sydney in 1893, and three years later I was a passenger on the first one to run from

A Sydney steam bus which ran from Enmore to Petersham in 1906

North Sydney to Spit Junction, Mosman. Its trolley pole was made from bamboo, and was not fixed in the middle of the roof but on one side. All the cars were painted in different fancy colours.'

Some styles

One morning in a Sydney museum I noticed a well-worn cushion in a display case. I would have passed it by but for the touching poem which had been painstakingly embroidered on it.

Advance Australia!

Come gentle babe
And with thy smile
A woman's dearest pains beguile
Come sweet infant, come and crown
Her days with blessings yet unknown.

Kylie Winkworth, assistant curator of costumes at the museum said:

'It's not really a cushion for sitting on, but a pincushion or pillow. They were popular in the early days of Australia and were embroidered by women with time on their hands or some important event in their lives to celebrate.

It's apparent that the words and motifs on this one were picked out first with coil-headed or round-headed pins and that in itself is significant. Pins were most expensive in the early nineteenth century and hard to get, so a pillow or pincushion like this was really a luxury and obviously a labour of love and care.

Apparently the woman who made it was expecting the birth of a child and the words "Advance Australia" reflected a growing feeling among people of the colony that one day it would be a nation instead of a forgotten penal colony and in her case, a better environment for her coming child to grow up in.

The embroidered date reads "June AD 1833" and it's obvious that not knowing the actual birth date she left a blank space. Bearing in mind the high mortality rate among mothers and the newborn then, you can't help wondering if the birth was successful.'

In the same section as the pincushion were a variety of clothes worn by women in colonial days, carefully preserved by families and donated to the museum: evening gowns, shoes, hats, and jewellery. But what did the women of early Australia wear underneath their ornate gowns and street clothes? Were they as well catered for as the women of today? I asked Kylie and got some surprises.

'Often, they didn't wear anything under the gowns at all, except numerous petticoats. In fact, it wasn't until 1850 that drawers were worn and only then by fashionable women. They were made from cotton and were open between the legs so that women would not suffer the inconvenience of having to take them down when they went to the toilet.

They became enclosed though in 1855 when crinolines came in, because a sudden fall or an upset with a crinoline might have exposed all!

By the 1900s women's underwear had lightened up somewhat. Now they wore a chemise next to the skin (it was a cross between a long singlet and a petticoat), and cotton drawers which were like long, loose underpants, tied around the waist with tape. A few years later lace was added to them for the first time. Until then women's underwear had been regarded in a very prim and proper way; any daintiness or prettiness suggested that the wearer was a tart who, in adding such fripperies intended that her unmentionables should be admired by others, probably men, who shouldn't have been allowed to see them, anyway.

On an even more intimate note, there were no manufactured sanitary products for women until 1932. Until then they had to make do with absorbent towels which could be laundered and used again and again.'

Both men and women's fashions were slow to change over the years, and it seems remarkable that the heavy, European-style clothing worn by Australian men in the nineteenth century—uncomfortably hot in summer—persisted well into the 1900s.

Even in 1956, Mr M. Solomons manager of the oldest-established ready-to-wear manufacturing business in New South Wales said:

'Men's fashions today are about the same as they were in 1913 or 1914: vents in the backs of coats, slanting side pockets and

Young men's clothing in the 1900s

bell-bottomed pants. There was just a slight change in the 1920s when Oxford bags came in with 22-inch bottoms or wider, and coats were longer, too, but there hasn't been much change, really. Except in the quality. At the turn of the century a man's suit lasted him six or seven years. Today, in 1956, it's half that . . . if you're lucky!'

In the 1930s men's dressing was formal, heavy and humourless. Three-piece suits (coats, pants and vests) were worn just about everywhere—sports coats were almost non-existent—and unless they were gardening or playing sport men wouldn't dream of going anywhere without a collar and tie. Some collars were stiff with wings, and in the summer threatened to asphyxiate the wearers, others, soft and detachable, were fastened to a shirt with two studs, a flat one at the back and a different kind with a press-in shaft at the front. The idea was that one could change the collar each day without changing the shirt. Inevitably, one was left with loads of leftover shirts or leftover collars, depending on which wore out first.

And hats were a must. One always had to be ready to take it off or at least raise it when one met a female.

Boots were worn more often than shoes, socks were usually woollen and when holes appeared in them they were darned by wives or mothers. Zippers were as yet unknown, of course and men's trousers had 'flies' in the front and were buttoned up, a cumbersome arrangement in an emergency. It brings to mind a child's riddle of the period:

'Is it cruel to stick pins into spiders?'

'No. You sew buttons on flies, don't you?'

Boys at school delighted in an annoying joke then; they would walk up to other boys and rip open their flies with a quick flick of the fingers. Predictably, it was called 'flying'.

Underpants were long, singlets had sleeves, socks were held up by suspenders, shirtsleeves by springy metal bands, and pants by braces, a much more comfortable form of suspension than belts which came in later.

Watch chains, a definite sign of respectability were worn across the vest together with one or two ornaments like sharks' teeth or small, silver spring-loaded sovereign cases, that is if anybody was lucky enough to possess a sovereign or two which were gold and worth £1 each. Telling the time was done with a flourish then; taking a gold or silver pocket watch out of a vest pocket and gravely inspecting it had a certain charm.

Older schoolboys wore knickerbockers to school. These were like plus fours, but not as baggy and were buttoned just below the knee with the socks pulled up over them. They were halfway between short and long pants and boys had two nicknames for them. One was 'applecatchers' and the other, which retained the second half of the word and replaced the first with another was highly descriptive, but is too vulgar to be repeated here.

Men's overcoats were of heavy material and in the lower price range at least were rather lumpy, but raglan-style raincoats with Prussian collars were also popular and well made. Scarves were worn with both styles and a popular kind were made from white silk or rayon. When knitted or crocheted they consisted of many one-inch squares with fringes of the same material at both ends of the scarves.

In the 1930s there were not only tailors for men, but also for women. Called 'tailoresses' they made costumes for women, tailored suits which followed the European mode. Of good quality they could be worn almost everywhere, and with a different blouse and jewellery could look like a different outfit altogether.

No horn-rimmed glasses for important executives then. Frames

A schoolboy of the 1920s in knickerbockers

were simple, in gold or silver and many spectacles had no frames or arms either. Just a small chain which fastened behind one ear and a spring clip which held the glasses in place on the nose, hence their name, pince nez.

Fancy deodorants were out in the 1930s. Just a little bay rum on the face perhaps after shaving, and the not-so-subtle smell of carbolic after the weekly bath with Lifebuoy soap, heavily advertised to keep BO (body odour) at bay. Coconut oil was popular for the hair.

A tugboat hand

George Wallace worked on boats all of his life, first on the northern rivers of New South Wales and then as a tugboat hand on Sydney Harbour. It was in the early 1900s in the days of sail.

I met George in the 1950s when he was eighty-five. Were they romantic times? Hardly, according to George:

'Talk about the "good old days"! Times were tough! I worked on the Clarence River for years, but I left in 1904 because all I was getting was £4 10s a month and I came to Sydney to do better, but things were crook on the waterfront then.

Young fellers couldn't become skippers until they had served a season with other skippers and they were all old men . . . masters. All old sailors and wonderful men . . . they taught us everything!

In those days the tugs lay alongside each other at Piermont waiting for news of ships. No wireless in them days. The skippers would go up to the post office and look at the orders. And talk about competition between the tugboats! The skipper might whisper to us, "I've been told there's a ship lying out there—" and the stoker would get steam up and away we'd go! But likely that somebody would have tied a rope with a tin can on it somewhere on our tug and the rattlin' would wake everybody up and they'd be off after us down the Harbour. Everybody wanted a ship!

Sometimes with steam up we'd go down as far as Jervis Bay and the damned ship would be somewhere to the east instead. Talk about competition!

You'd sail up alongside a ship and the master'd say, "How much a ton?" "Eighteen pence," you'd yell back. "How about you?" he'd ask another tug. "A shilling a ton" the skipper might say, wanting the work.

Well! I've seen them tow big ships from Jervis Bay to their berths in the Harbour sometimes for fourpence a ton!

At that time all the ships used were five-masted, fore-and-aft rigged. None were square-rigged at all, except in the case of one family who owned some. All of theirs were painted black—the hulls, that is—and they sailed out here every six months, all square-rigged in every mast.

With all their royals flying they were the prettiest sight in the world, especially with two together. No yacht race anywhere could compare with that, and they used to have races, too.

The discipline on the big ships was very good. You never heard of any trouble, although the food was—well, just food and that was all . . . corned beef and a loaf of bread and sailors had to put up with it. That was all we got on tugboats, too.

I remember one Christmas Day we had to go lookin' for a ship, and for lunch all we got was corned beef and bread and butter. We was lucky to get the butter and you had to eat it where you could.

There were no set hours for working on Sydney Harbour in them days. You had to work when there *was* work, night or day. No double time, anything like that and you were paid by the job you done. If a ship sailed at night us tugboat hands got half-a-crown each for it. Even the skipper and the engineer only got three bob each.

I remember once we were working at two in the morning and the owner come down. He says, "Oh well, you won't need to be early tomorrow morning, boys. Four o'clock in the morning will do." That was how you got your orders then.

You know, there was plenty of smuggling about on the sailing ships in them days . . . there was hundreds of things you could smuggle and the water police—they had to row about. No motor launches then. There were four men to a boat and they had to row from Circular Quay to Blackwattle Bay and just about everywhere. They were always looking for smugglers.

I remember one funny thing that happened. See, the cooks on the sailing ships saved all the grease from the galleys, and they sold it to people who went round the different ships in port buying it. Well, a cook on one of them asked me if I would take a cask of grease ashore for him. I said, "No, it's not in my line" but a mate of mine, old Dick West took it ashore and got a couple of pounds for doing it. We helped him lift it up on to the wharf at Erskine Street where we were all waiting for work. The water police were there too, sniffing about.

Then a lorry came down to pick up the cask. Dick had been told by the ship's cook to watch out for it and he said to the police, "Come on, you hefty fellers, give us a hand with this cask" and they helped him to lift it on to the lorry which drove off with it.

Sydney water police in the 1890s

Well, a couple of days after a feller we knew came down and said, "You know what was in that barrel?" "What?" we asked. "Opium," he says. "It was worth millions!"

The coppers were there and they helped Dick put it on the bloody lorry!'

Remembering it all, George roared with laughter—and who could blame him? At the age of eighty-five what was life worth without an illicit memory or two?

Percy Benison, cartoonist

Percy was 86-years-old when I met him in the 1960s. During his working life he had been a freelance cartoonist and artist with Australia's leading newspapers. The passing of time had given him a new perspective on his life and the difficulties of working in a creative field. Looking back on it in retirement he could regard it now with a wry smile . . .

'I remember my first job, it was with the Melbourne *Truth*. The editor called me up and said, "I want you to go down to the morgue."

I said, "The morgue?"

"Yes," he said. "There's a cove down there who blew the top of his head off. We can't get a picture of him any other way. Go down to the morgue and draw him."

I didn't like the idea much but I wended my way across Princes Bridge and down to the morgue, a funny little house on the banks of the Yarra. I knocked at the door and a big copper came out and asked what I wanted.

I said, "My editor has sent me down here to draw a bloke you've got on one of the slabs." "Right," he said and took me to him. It was my first drawing of a corpse. I finished it and I tell you it didn't take me long to get out of there. The year was 1901.

That started me off and after that I went all over the place . . . did divorces, sketched ladies of pleasure in Little Lon, which used to be Melbourne's brothel area, with ladies squatting on cane chairs outside their little cottages on both sides of the street, and illustrations as well.

In those days—unlike today—funny sketches always had captions underneath them in order to explain the joke, and they were often long and laboured, but as long as the caption was right and the drawing good, it was considered acceptable.

I remember the first one I did. Money was scarce at the time and mine brought in the huge sum of £2 2s. It showed a dirty old tramp sitting in a dump reading a newspaper. He was talking to another tramp and he said in the caption: "I see here where a feller died after drinking a gallon of whisky" and the other says, "Oh? What did he die of?"

While living in Melbourne around the turn of the century and drawing for the *Truth* I had a studio in a place called Queen's Walk in Collins Street, right opposite the Town Hall and next door to the Savage Club. I was frightfully poor . . . in fact, all artists were in those days. I had to sleep on the floor or on a box I'd covered with some borrowed felt. But I was happy, and as things improved was able to buy a chair and other things.

By and by I was able to sell some of my stuff to the *Bulletin*. They accepted more and more of it along with artwork from people like Norman Lindsay who was a top artist in those days. He did quite a lot, B.E. Minns also and old timers like George Lambert. They were an interesting lot, but of course they were in Sydney, five hundred miles away.

Later on, I got an offer by the *Bulletin* to go to Sydney, and of course I did.

I drew continually for the *Bulletin* for the next sixty years. Not a bad record. I was also a political cartoonist for the *Evening News*. I drew for Sydney Ure Smith publications . . . the *Guardian* . . . in fact, I worked for most of the papers in Sydney.

My ambition as a young man was to draw as well as that great English artist, Phil May. He was brought out here by the *Bulletin* to draw political cartoons. He became world famous and was a great draftsman. He did all his drawings in detail in pencil first, then rubbed out all the lines he thought were not necessary before inking them in. I modelled my work on his and was partially successful, I think. May was a genius.

Much has been written about the *Bulletin* and the people who ran it in the early days. Well, I can tell you that with all my years of experience there is only one *Bulletin* and working there was like working with your own family. When you walked in they were really pleased to see you.

I took a sketch in once and the editor looked up from his desk at the young man standing in front of him and said, "What do *you* want?"

"I have a funny sketch," I said nervously.

He took it, looked at it, smiled and then broke into a chuckle. "Very good," he said. That was all he said but the news was good and so was the money. The sketch showed a woman in one of those very long dresses of the day. It was dragging on the footpath behind her. The woman said to her male companion, “I have my new dress on. Do you like it?”

The man said, “Yes. Any microbe that skirt misses is not worth catching.” That was the joke.

My drawing days are over now, not because I'm tired but because my eyes are . . . they don't see things like they used to.

Only ten years ago I was asked to do a series of drawings for a children's weekly comic called *The Lone Avenger*. Kids everywhere loved him . . . he was masked and a good Samaritan, tracking down baddies, etcetera.

The series became very successful. In fact I was told that it had the largest circulation of any kids' comic in Australia! I drew it for quite a while. I had to because the chap who started it was in jail. What tickled me was that all the kids of eight and nine who eagerly waited for it to come out each week didn't know that the adventures of the Lone Avenger were the product of an old man, 75-years-old . . . namely myself!'

Three professional women

The precise, elderly woman told me her name was Miss Roberts, and when I asked for her first name she repeated 'Miss Roberts' so I didn't ask again. She had been a school teacher for most of her life, and obviously had been known as 'Miss Roberts' to generations of school children, and that was enough. Her working years were now well behind her, but she hardly seemed to have left the classroom. She held herself erect in her chair while her lips seemed ready to purse in disapproval at the first hint of familiarity or perhaps to soften if something pleased her. In response to another question she told me that her teaching career had begun at a very bad time.

'It was in 1918, the time of the terrible Spanish flu epidemic . . . there were three recurrences of it. The schools closed . . . so did the churches and theatres . . . everybody had to be in the open air as much as possible. Victory celebrations were cancelled and wartime price controls were enforced to prevent profiteering in medicine. The serum laboratories provided three million doses of a bacterial vaccine but it was doubtful whether it was effective.

There was a lot of panic, but mind you much of it was fright! People you knew used to cross over to the opposite side of the street when they saw you and you couldn't blame them!

I had no knowledge of nursing but I was instructed by my department to help a doctor and I went round with him giving out jelly and soup and things like that. I saw one man die and I'll never forget it. People at that time all had to wear masks—it was compulsory—and had to go to the Town Hall to get sprayed. Various treatments were suggested for the flu: aspirin three times a day, menthol and eucalyptus sniffed regularly, and up in Queensland oil of turpentine was recommended as a preventative and that led to a run on chemists' stocks but apparently none of them did much good.

I knew a great number of people who died and many of them were doctors. Twelve thousand Australians died before the epidemic eased.

I was a school teacher for thirty-seven years until a little while ago, and I met only three children I couldn't do anything with! Most were all right. From my long experience I would say that what a teacher needs most is tact, sympathy, discretion and a certain firmness . . . but sympathy is most essential. You must see things from a child's point of view and you must acknowledge sometimes that you, the teacher may be wrong! I think children have changed and lack the opportunities that we had say, when I was a child in the 1870s and 1880s, because they haven't the home life or parents' interest or any of the things we had as children.

Like when I came home from school, Mother was always there . . . when he got home my father would want to know how I got on at school that day and so on. Now, parents—many of them—are just too busy to care!

Another thing, children today don't get to read good books to help them develop their gifts of expression. They seem to have very little gift of expression. That's the situation today!'

Another school teacher, Miss A.E. Turner was of an even earlier vintage—equally authoritative but more quietly spoken.

'I began my teaching career at Miss Baxter's private school for girls in Darlinghurst, Sydney in 1899. It was called "Argyle". I was twenty-one, it was my first teaching job, and while my father didn't object to me getting my BA at Sydney University—I was one of the first women to do so—he didn't approve when I told him I wanted to be a teacher and go to work. He gave his permission though finally, and I was honoured to be the first teacher taken on at Argyle who had not been trained by Miss Baxter herself. The school which she had started in 1872 had a fine history, and was one of many then which provided secondary education instead of public high schools.

Miss Baxter had been a pioneer in women's education and was determined that her girls would get the same opportunities as boys, an idea which was considered outrageous then. When she opened her school, girls were not admitted to universities; in fact it was not until 1881 that the appropriate act was passed allowing them to do so.'

Miss Baxter sounded like an interesting woman but I wanted to hear from Miss Turner about herself. Before I could get on with it—

Miss A.E. Turner

'At that time of course, girls were not expected to have brains, and if they did, certainly not to use them and when Miss Baxter insisted on every girl learning mathematics, she lost many prospective pupils; their fathers claimed that they would never marry if they had a knowledge of such things.

It wasn't until the bank failures of the 1890s that women had any opportunity of taking part in public life, then the first tearoom in Sydney run by a woman was opened, also the first florist's shop with a woman in charge. Indeed, it wasn't until many years after that, that any girl was employed by a bank, and that was due to the fact that all the men were away fighting overseas in World War I.

I was paid £80 a year as a teacher at Miss Baxter's school, I taught there for thirteen years and the salary remained unchanged. I know I was disgusted when some of my former pupils who had been trained in the school as secretaries and shorthand typists went out and got themselves jobs at £5 a week.

She believed in hard work. When Empire Day was introduced, public schools got a holiday but she said the best way to serve the empire was doing our usual work, so there was no holiday.'

Whether I wanted to or not I was getting a clear picture of Miss Baxter. Miss Turner added:

'She always dressed in black with a little standup collar and a stiff white collar inside it. She wore the same all the year round because she used to say, "What keeps out the heat in summer can keep it in in winter."

Her interest in women's rights was one of the driving forces in her life. Before starting her school in 1872 she had sought advice about the curriculum from her former Latin tutor, a well-known educationist named Professor Charles Badham. He said, "Teach them Latin but don't bother about maths. They can always call their maids to add up their bills." It must have infuriated her and made her all the more determined to defend the rights of women.'

I thought I'd heard enough about Miss Baxter for a while and asked Miss Turner (who was eighty-nine) what life was like when she was a young teacher in Darlinghurst just before the turn of the century.

'Life was very congenial. I used to walk to the school from the top of William Street, and on Sundays I attended St John's Church of England. It was a very fashionable church and was often called Thomson and Giles's showroom because the people who attended were considered to be the best-dressed in Sydney. They rode up in their carriages and although they've gone, the church is still there bordering on Kings Cross, and what's left of the beautiful houses like Alberto Terrace are hidden behind shops today.

In the early days nobody called it Kings Cross, it was simply "the top of William Street" and there were cable trams running up and down, and out to Rushcutters Bay. The houses in that part of Sydney were beautiful then . . . three-storeyed with lovely lawns in front, and Elizabeth Bay House was only one of many grand houses overlooking Sydney Harbour.

Miss Baxter's school stood where St Margarets Hospital is now. Ninety girls attended. Many day girls rode up each morning in carriages and pairs, and some boarders came from distant places. One I remember came from the Northern Territory and didn't go home for three years because the journey took three weeks. The school was in Albion Street which used to be called Doctors' Row because so many of them had rooms there. Miss Baxter was, I think the first school principal to introduce school uniforms for girls in Australia . . . black boots and socks and grey dresses summer and winter.

I taught Latin, French, English history, geography and maths at Argyle, and when the government decided to play a bigger part in secondary education, I left Argyle and applied for one of forty teaching positions made available in high schools. I was one of the successful applicants chosen from a field of three thousand. I was appointed assistant mistress in history and English at Fort Street Girls' High School. The salary was up to £250 a year . . . more than three times the salary Miss Baxter paid me.

I'm glad I began my career with Miss Baxter, she set a standard.'

Miss Turner retired as assistant headmistress of Fort Street Girls' High School nearly a quarter of a century later in 1938.

By now it was apparent that Miss Baxter had been one of Australia's first feminists and a woman of great determination. It was obvious that she had also become Miss Turner's alter ego, and I wished I could have interviewed her instead. In a way, with Miss Turner's help, I supposed I had.

Like Miss Turner, Molly Gant was born 'at the top of William Street' in the 1880s. She belonged to a well-to-do family and at the time when it was believed that a knowledge of etiquette and other social graces were more important to a girl than a well-rounded education, her parents ignored the convention, made sure she was educated properly and had her taught piano. In the fullness of time she graduated as a professional pianist and teacher, and because of her skills at the keyboard and her favoured family background, was sought after to play at select gatherings of Sydney society.

Recalling one of these glittering occasions, Molly, a chuckling, alert woman of eighty-nine years, said:

'I think the happiest night I ever spent was when I played at Cranbrook for the governor, Lord Chelmsford and Lady Chelmsford. Cranbrook is a school today but then—in 1913—it was the governor's residence. The reason for the party was to entertain some of Sydney's notables, and many people I knew socially when I was growing up attended. It was such an elegant occasion: the ladies beautifully and expensively dressed in their long glittering gowns, as the men, moustached and wearing tails swept them around the floor to a fast rendition of "The Blue Danube".

They were snobbish times of course. Now I had been brought up to ignore anything which might offend me in any way and during the evening, one of the women guests, who almost lived at my home when my family was entertaining caught sight of me seated at the piano. She cut me dead! I was *working* there!

Soon afterwards a servant announced, "Would the ladies and gentlemen now go to the verandah while the vice-regal party has its supper?" and with that Lord Chelmsford, followed by his aide walked the length of the ballroom to me and said, "May I have the honour to take you to supper?"

It was a wonderful experience! No wonder I remember it! Afterwards, my snobbish friend was glad to come up to me and say, "Why, hello, Molly. I didn't know it was you!"

Ah, they were wonderful times in Sydney then. Looking back I remember the wonderful dances given by Mr Arthur Allen of Edgecliff. At one of them I had the honour to play for the Prince of Wales, later the Duke of Windsor.

I was practice accompanist for the famous Irish tenor John McCormack. That was about 1912. He was a charming man, very reserved and very quiet. I remember the first time I played his favourite song for him. It was "Macushla". He patted me on the head and said, "That's just the way I want it." He always practised in the big room at the Hotel Australia. It had a full-length grand piano. I practised with him before all his Sydney concerts, but his accompanist on stage was Ernest Sykes, *the* accompanist in Sydney at the time.

I also accompanied Dame Clara Butt, the international contralto. Impressed on my memory is the exquisite sound of her voice when she sang her most famous song, "The Lost Chord". Her voice sounded like an organ.'

Undoubtedly, the greatest experience in Molly's life was when she met and became practise pianist for the greatest soprano in the world, Dame Nellie Melba.

'Dame Nellie Melba was an amazing woman, very disciplined and expected everybody around her to be the same. She was born in Burnley, Victoria in 1861, and belonged to a very musical family. She was taught piano and organ but when she played and sang publicly a critic, whom she respected told her to forget the instruments and to concentrate on singing instead.

She did, had her voice trained overseas with a famous teacher and when she made her debut in 1887 changed her name, Helen Porter Mitchell to "Nellie Melba". Success followed success. In 1904 she gave a Command Performance at Buckingham Palace and in 1920 was made a Dame of the British Empire. Her repertoire included twenty-five operas and when she sang, anywhere in the world, houses sold out.

I'll never forget the day I met her. It was in 1903 and at that time she was, as they say, at the height of her powers. My aunt, Kate Slattery, a well-known dramatic soprano was a friend of Melba's, and we were shown up to her rooms at the Hotel Australia, and my aunt and Melba made a fuss of each other. Then Aunt Kate introduced me and told Melba I was a pianist. She asked me the name of my teacher.

When I told her, her face lit up. "Why, I studied with her as well!"

Nellie Melba, 1903

she exclaimed, and it put us on a good footing at once. She said she would like me to play for her but first offered us some refreshment. "What would you like, Kitty?" she asked my aunt.

"I will have a ginger beer," my aunt said.

Melba looked down her nose and was on her sophisticated high horse at once. "Ginger beer!" she said with raised eyebrows. "What kind of drink is *that*?"

My aunt, who had been a friend of Melba's for a long time wasn't perturbed. "Now then, Nellie," she said. "You know very well what ginger beer is . . . it's a cordial of the day."

Melba turned to me. "How about you, Molly?"

I was still nervous. "A ginger ale, thank you," I said, thinking I had better make mine slightly different.

Dame Nellie said, "Well, I think I'll have a cocktail."

It was the first time I had ever heard of one. A maid was called, given our orders then Dame Nellie gave her all kinds of things she wanted in her cocktail. The maid left, but soon afterwards returned with "Excuse me, Madame, but I believe I've forgotten one of the ingredients for your cocktail."

Melba barked, "Where is your head? Where are your ears? Go outside and think!"

That was the kind of woman Melba was. She could give you all the joy in the world but could be very hard on people, too.

Then Madame said she would like to hear me play. I sat down at the grand piano and played “Ah! Fors e lui” (“Can it Be He?”) from *La Traviata*, and a few little ballads, but Dame Nellie wasn’t keen on ballads; she preferred opera.

She and my aunt gossiped for a while and then she took us into a room nearby where a woman was sewing real diamonds and pearls on to an evening gown for Madame. She was locked in because of the value of the jewels. It was a magnificent gown and Madame wore it to a recital that night.

I was very lucky because my audition with Madame was successful and she appointed me as her practice pianist. I also had to play when she auditioned young untried sopranos. She was very tough on all of them, yelling sometimes, “Have you got any money to go overseas and study? No? Then you’d better hurry up and get some because it’s a waste of time without it!”

I think she was testing them to see if they could stand up to what she had been through as a young singer herself.

On the other hand, she was most generous to people down on their luck, but never talked about it. I had some private luncheons with her, had long talks with her too and she was always very nice to me.

What can one say about Melba’s voice, except that it was the voice of a bird . . . absolutely magnificent! One could never hope to hear one better and I have never heard one better and I am eighty-nine years old. But she was a solitary person, liked to be alone and hated being thwarted. She and my aunt were different kinds of singers. The latter was not a professional but fulfilled many public engagements in Sydney and Melbourne and I remember that when she sang once for the poor in Bendigo, miners threw bits of gold on the stage. She was loved, and loved as a singer.

Melba, on the other hand was admired . . . tremendously so, and her frocking was as magnificent as her voice. I never knew her to be nervous, even before a big performance. She always showed great poise and when off-stage was singing all the time, softly to herself.

I was her pianist for some months. When the opera season finished, she returned overseas and I’m sorry to say I never saw her again.

Admittedly, Dame Nellie had a reputation for being irascible, determined and overbearing. She was a typical prima donna and her respect for her voice, which she regarded as a precious instrument dictated her way of life. In her later years, like many great singers, she was reluctant to retire and gave so many farewell concerts around the world, people wondered when they would stop. She died in 1931 aged seventy.’

Those magnificent men . . . those intrepid women

Let's face it: flying is not as much fun as it used to be. First, the dodgy ride to the airport where we're quizzed, numbered, frisked and X-rayed, force-fed into long metal tubes and strapped into seats which must have been designed for humans with one buttock and no arms or elbows. Then a screaming take-off with nothing left to look forward to but airline food, a reminder that the pet cats and dogs we left at home will probably be eating better than us!

It's not much better up front where the 'pilots' are. The daring young men of yesteryear in their helmets and goggles, flying by the seats of their pants, sitting in draughty cockpits and watching shaky compass needles have gone and in their place, uniformed attendants lazing about watching a visual display unit and letting computers do most of the work!

In short, the 'good old days', the romantic, adventurous days when a flight was called 'a flip', when wooden propellers were swung by hand and a spluttering engine could mean the difference between fame and oblivion are over, but fortunately the pilots who flew for pleasure or profit in the exciting 1920s and 1930s were still around in the 1950s and 1960s and were able to describe, first-hand what it was like to fly when Australian aviation was young.

'I'm Arthur Jones, and I'm eighty-two years old. I made my first solo flight in 1911, only eight years after the Wright Brothers made theirs. A friend and I built the plane. It was a monoplane like the *Bleriot* which was the first plane to cross the English Channel.

Ours was powered by an ordinary car engine. We were able to cut down on the weight here and there by substituting lighter materials. The wings were made from wood and covered with calico and had wooden struts. We used bamboo too, and the wheels were off a pushbike.

After much experiment I flew it off the ground to a height of twenty-five feet.'

Jones was a novice compared with Lawrence Hargrave who, twenty-eight years earlier in 1883 was already proving the possibility of man-made flight with the use of models. Born in England in 1850 he came out to Australia at the age of sixteen, became an engineer and experimented with box kites—he had eighty of them—which he flew in Sydney and at Stanwell Park on the south coast of New South Wales. His tests would have far-reaching results, paving the way with his 'stable support surface' for the world's first really airworthy aeroplanes.

(The Wright Brothers aeroplane, on the other hand, first flown publicly in 1909 flew in hops, or 'fits and starts' as one critic described it and was extremely difficult to control.)

French designers, in particular adopted Hargrave's stable support surface in their aircraft and another of his inventions, a radial rotary engine, years ahead of its time represented another starting point for overseas companies. It was the basis for the Gnome aircraft engine used in planes during World War I.

Hargrave and Jones were but two of many Australians who, with only an elementary knowledge of aerodynamics and with varying degrees of success designed or built planes and braved the skies in them, but no doubt because of a peculiarly Australian attitude—one which persists today—that anybody who attempted anything beyond the aspirations of the rank-and-file should not be admired but ignored, few are remembered now.

Edward Hallstrom (later Sir Edward Hallstrom, 'the father of Australian refrigeration') combined with George A. Taylor in 1909 in the adventurous business of flying box kites and designing gliders. In fact Hallstrom, at the age of twenty-one, built a wooden glider, climbed into it and persuaded reluctant spectators to push it over a cliff at Narrabeen, New South Wales. The flight was moderately successful and Ted became one of the first Australians to fly.

During World War I there was an urgent need for better planes and heroic pilots to fly them, but since the war was fought on foreign fields, its details have no place here. However, when it was over a new breed of Australian fliers emerged, young people who, together with former wartime pilots joined the newly-formed Australian Aero Club and flew from aerodromes around Australia.

At this time flying, in the public mind was thought to be glamorous and exciting, although only a few Australians could afford to learn to fly. Dual instruction cost £3 an hour. The basic wage then was about £3 a week and since it took a minimum of eight hours dual before even a smart pupil could be tested for his 'A' (non-commercial) licence, learning to fly and going solo afterwards at £2 an hour was generally a hobby for the rich.

Meg Skelton, Margaret Kently and Marie Richardson, three of Australia's earliest women pilots, were the first of the few in a man's world more than sixty years ago when Mascot aerodrome was little more than a cow paddock.

Meg, who joined the Aero Club in 1928 and went solo the following year told me, 'Mascot looked like a reclaimed tip and the takeoff strip was changed daily. Kerosene tins were moved about as markers for take-offs and landings.'

'You didn't mention the steers,' Margaret Kently reminded her. 'At that time Mascot was leased by a man named Nigel Love and there was a slaughterhouse nearby. The animals were brought down from Queensland and they used to escape sometimes and wander about. They were pretty wild and we had to dodge them on landing or taking off. Sometimes, they charged the planes!'

The women, like all Aero Club members then flew in De Havilland Gypsy Moths (DH 60's). They were small single-engined biplanes with two cockpits, one behind the other and were of wooden construction with linen-covered wings which could be folded when in a hangar. Their cruising speed was 70 mph.

Pilots extolled the beauty of the Gypsy Moth and no wonder. It is likely that few small planes of the period seemed so eager to fly, looked as light or were so aerodynamically pleasing as the Moth. If the description seems a little over the top, it is echoed by Marie Richardson:

'When I was in the open cockpit of a Gypsy Moth, alone, thousands of feet above the city, I felt I owned everything I could see and the Moth and I were one. From the moment of take-off, when it lifted off the grass and later when we returned and I made my approach with engine cut back and with a slight adjustment or two on the stick and then the bump of a gentle landing . . . it was wonderful every time!

I remember I was on my way to a music lesson one day in 1919 and I saw Ross and Keith Smith flying overhead in their Vickers Vimy at the end of their record-breaking flight from England: I decided there and then that when I grew up I would be a pilot, too. I just knew I would!'

A DH60 Gypsy Moth getting airborne

Margaret Kently said:

'For me, every aspect of flying in the 1930s was exciting. It was a time of waking up early, looking out of my bedroom window at smokestacks to see the strength and direction of the wind, then if conditions were favourable, a quick trip to Mascot, into a Moth and up, up into the sky for perhaps a flight to the North Shore to do a few lazy circuits over my home. What an experience with the blue sky all around and fluffy white clouds and Sydney—as it was then—beneath me.

On the way back to Mascot, perhaps a spin with the earth going round and round . . . then at the last minute, controls centralised and a pull out at 1500 feet, and I was flying level again. It was a feeling you couldn't get anywhere else!

Even walking around a Moth on the ground was exciting . . . the only movement the rudder perhaps shifting a little with the breeze and everything about it so light . . . except the engine, of course. One became friendly with a Moth . . . you were part of it and it was part of you as soon as you climbed into the cockpit. It was a bit like having a dog . . . there was a closeness—

We used to fly cross-country to air pageants in Melbourne and different country towns. We found our way with ordinary road maps and by following railway lines and main roads. The range of the planes was short and often we put down in paddocks and filled up

Women pilots of the 1930s about to provide an aerial escort for Amy Johnson on her arrival in Sydney. From left to right: Meg Skelton, Bobby Terry, Evelyn Follett, Alice Upfold, Phillis Arnott, Freda Deaton

with petrol from four-gallon cans which we had to hoist up to the tanks ourselves.

I remember flying to the opening of the Wagga aerodrome by the Duke of Gloucester. The Air Force was there with six Hawker Demon fighters . . . there were twelve other planes, including ours from Sydney and the Victorian Aero Club, and together they represented most of the small planes in Australia at that time.'

Despite the fulsome praise though there was a downside to flying a DH 60. Meg Skelton says:

'It was always a joy in good weather, but flying in rain—and we did a lot of it—wasn't pleasant. The Gypsy Moth had its petrol tank set between the two upper wings at the top of the centre section, above and forward of the pilot. It had grooves in it which sloped down to its trailing edge and anybody who has experienced water torture will know what it was like to have a constant splash of rain hit you right in the middle of the forehead between your helmet and goggles. It was like being continually pelted with pebbles!

But it was wonderful when friends were coming home from England by ship. We used to fly out to the Heads to meet them then fly in formation alongside the ships as they sailed up the Harbour. What a welcome!

We did the same for Amy Johnson when she flew into Sydney at the end of her record-breaking flight from England in 1930. We provided an aerial escort all the way to Mascot!

In 1937 they put lights in the control tower at Mascot and we thought it was the beginning of too much control so we transferred to Camden where our friends, the Onslows, had a small aerodrome of their own. We used to take off from there, chase cows in the paddocks or fly along the Hume Highway and see how close we could get to cars without touching their roofs with our wheels.'

Life was much the same for amateur pilots at Essendon Aerodrome on the outskirts of Melbourne. There were few rules. Power dives over the roof of the Aero Clubhouse, formation flying along the tarmac so low and with wingtips so close to the hangars that they made the doors rattle, were part of a carefree, innocent time before the bureaucrats moved in with a fistful of regulations. Inevitably, the lazy days were almost over as flying became more sophisticated.

It was in the 1930s that the Clancy brothers, Bill, Allan and Jack decided to design, build and fly an aeroplane. Unusual, because they knew nothing about the skills required, had not flown before and it was a matter of the blind leading the blind. They had seen pictures of a parasol-type single-seater monoplane though and Bill, who was an engineer started from scratch and drew the plans.

They built the plane from wood in a garage at Rosebery in Sydney and called it the *Clancy Sky Baby.* They all got minimum flying instruction (Jack who was sixteen years old couldn't afford more than a couple of hours), and each flew the plane without mishap. Powered with a modified Henderson motorbike engine it was cheap to run. With petrol at 1s 6d a gallon, it cost only about 4s (40c) for an hour's flying.

That was more than sixty years ago. The *Sky Baby* should have been forgotten or have found a modest place in Australian aviation history, but not so. Six more were built over the years, and in the 1980s American fliers took an interest. Jack Clancy sent them plans and they built and flew another. It was intended for an American museum, but Jack persuaded them to lend it to Australia, and now it resides in Sydney's Powerhouse Museum.

There's more. Jack, now seventy-seven, has outlived his two older brothers, and has hand-built another *Sky Baby* from the original plans! He is a retired aircraft ground engineer and has added some new features and used techniques which were not available before: dacron has replaced linen on the wings and control surfaces, the wooden airframe is held together by modern adhesives (furniture glue was used in the original), and the old Henderson motorbike engine has been replaced by a Volkswagen engine which Jack ingeniously reduced from four cylinders to two to provide the amount of power he wanted. The original airframe was built from oregon. Jack has done the same with this one, and it looks almost the same as the old.

'The *Sky Baby* has no vices. It weighs 296 pounds, cruises at 60 miles an hour, and lands at 27. I fly it, my daughter who is a flying instructor flies it and soon my two grand-daughters will be, too. Unfortunately, I can't fly it in Sydney, and finding suitable airstrips in the country is a problem.'

The professionals

They flew in all weathers, took incredible risks and flew where nobody had flown before. Often, they were called reckless, impractical, of risking their lives and those of their companions for nothing except the hope of creating or breaking another record.

They were the trailblazers, addicted to adventure and excitement. Up there, with their eyes on a distant horizon they knew that they were the first of many; that there would come a time when millions like them would fly but without near-empty petrol tanks, poor navigational aids and a continual fight to ward off sleep.

Sir Charles Kingsford Smith was arguably the greatest of all. In the eyes of the public he fitted the image of the intrepid pilot exactly: had a hawklike countenance, a confident grin, and although he was a man of small stature he stood tall in the minds of his admirers, broke record after record and gave the world the excitement it craved.

Born in 1897, he seemed destined to fly. He flew with the Royal Flying Corps in World War I, won a DFC for shooting down enemy aircraft and after the armistice began flying commercially at Mascot. In 1928 he flew around Australia in the record time of ten days, five hours; and it marked the beginning of a spectacular career of epic flights across the world. He notched up more firsts than any other pilot in the world and sometimes against almost impossible odds.

In 1928, with co-pilot Charles Ulm he flew a newly-acquired Avro 10 three-engined monoplane, *Southern Cross*, from Oakland, California to Brisbane in 83 hours, 38 minutes, and was greeted by 65 000 people (and later, by 300 000 in Sydney).

A record-breaking flight from Sydney to New Zealand, a distance of 1630 miles was undertaken in such terrible weather that it took

Sir Charles Kingsford Smith

the combined strength of 'Smithy' and Ulm to hold the controls and keep *Southern Cross* in the air. They were successful though with a record-breaking flight time of fourteen-and-a-half hours.

They flew back to Sydney soon afterwards against equally-strong headwinds and landed at Richmond, New South Wales after dark with car headlights illuminating the runway. They had three gallons of petrol sufficient for only another ten minutes of flying left in their tanks.

In 1929, Smithy helped develop Australian National Airways and set out for London in *Southern Cross* in search of planes and pilots for the new company. In doing so he broke the Sydney–London record with a flying time of twelve days, eighteen hours.

Ulm returned to Australia afterwards to help organise the airline and Smithy flew from London to Newfoundland, broke another record, and was given a ticker-tape parade in New York. He also had lunch with the president of the US.

Other notable flights followed, and by 1934 he had made the first crossing of the Pacific in a single-engine aircraft, his Lockheed Altair, *Lady Southern Cross.* (Tragically, whilst flying from California to Honolulu, Ulm disappeared after a final radio message: 'I think we're going into the drink.')

Smithy clipped the flying times off several records—including his own—and by now he and *Southern Cross* had found a lasting place in the saga of world aviation.

There seemed to be no stopping him, but in 1935, in London, unwell and against the advice of friends and family he decided to fly back to Australia in *Lady Southern Cross.* With a flight engineer, Tommy Pethybridge he took off from London in November, was reported flying over Calcutta, Burma and the Bay of Bengal and then an ominous silence. The remains of the two men were never found.

Sir Charles Kingsford Smith is remembered as a man who followed his star, who carved paths in the air where none had been before, but such excursions were costly and at a time when corporate sponsorship was virtually unknown he often had to scratch to make ends meet.

Using his famous name and flying *Southern Cross* he went barnstorming in Australia and New Zealand, following the well-established Australian practice in hard times of 'doing anything for a quid' and took people up for joy flights in the 'Old Bus'. Harold Affleck, an aircraft engineer describes what happened when Smithy took his big Avro 10 up-country in the 1930s to make some money from joy flights:

'I remember a terrible day when we flew into Kempsey at five o'clock in the afternoon. It was pouring with rain, but we got down all right in a paddock which the organisers had arranged for us. We left *Southern Cross* with our night watchman and went into town to stay overnight in a pub.

In the early hours of the morning the watchman in the plane woke up and thought he could hear water running. He looked out of the window and to his horror saw a sheet of water around *Southern Cross.* Already, it was lapping at the wheels! He got out, and with a lot of difficulty worked his way across the paddock to a farmhouse, woke up the people there, borrowed a horse and rode a couple of miles at breakneck speed to a phone and woke Smithy at the hotel.

Smithy got us all up and we tore out to the paddock. By the time we got there the water had risen over the wheels! It was obvious that the "Old Bus" had to be moved quickly to higher ground, so Smithy hopped in and tried to start the engines, but the air was so humid only one of the three would go, and one didn't have enough power to move the plane.

Southern Cross *(the 'Old Bus') 'We were always pushing the damn thing'*

"We'll have to get a bullock team," Smithy said.

So we worked our way over to the farmhouse, woke everybody up again and luckily were able to get one at once from a neighbouring farmer, but by the time we got back to the paddock with it, the water was too deep for the bullocks; they were actually swimming! The rain was still pelting down.

"All right," Smithy said, in his usual, practical way. "Our only hope is the engines. This time we've got to make it."

I'd like to say that this time the engines started, but that only happens at the movies. Smithy got the same one going again, but not the others and with the engine roaring full blast and almost swimming ourselves we were able to push *Southern Cross* to higher ground. Somehow, we always seemed to be pushing the damned thing.

The rain lasted for three days and the whole area around the plane was a lake. It subsided finally though, we dried out the engines and got on with barnstorming.

I was with Smithy for four years in Australia and New Zealand, and I should tell you that I never knew him to make a bad landing. He was a born flier, but I'm afraid a poor businessman. That's why, despite his great historic flights he had to turn to joy-riding and sometimes take on jobs which normally he would not have done. I remember once he arranged to take the boys in Westmead Boys' Band up for a flight at Mascot.

At that time there was a Sydney photographer named Ray Vaughan who often flew with us and took pictures from the air. On this occasion he thought it would be a good idea to take some novel aerial pictures of Sydney from a different angle, and after talking with him about it, we roped him down with his camera on top of the wing of *Southern Cross*, right in the middle. Then I hopped in with the boys and Smithy took off.

However, soon after we left the ground I realised that something was wrong. Instead of climbing and heading for the city, Smithy made a very careful flat turn, then flew very slowly around the aerodrome and landed.

I got out and found that poor Ray Vaughan, still roped to the top of the wing was in a bad way. In fact, he had nearly lost his life, because he was lying in the vacuum over the top of the wing and was unable to breathe. At the same time his body was stopping the slipstream from the middle engine getting to the rudder and elevators. Smithy could hardly get any lift, had restricted control, and had to go around flat and land.'

Joe Taylor was in the aircraft industry for fifty years and like Harold Affleck earned his living for some years as a mechanic and maintenance engineer with a barnstorming crew who took people up for joy flights all over New South Wales.

'It was during the Depression and the pilot was a well-known man, Les Holden. The aircraft we used was a DH4 biplane with a little Avian as a support plane. The price per head for joy flights started at £1, but then as things got worse we came down to ten shillings, and finally, when we were on our uppers at Moree, down to 2s 6d.

But we kept on doing it, flying to any big country town where there was an important race meeting or other special entertainment. Before we landed we usually dropped a message asking local people to point to where a suitable landing spot was. If it was a paddock we usually got somebody with a truck to drive over it, to see how deep the wheels sank into it and whether we could land safely. Even when we got down to 2s 6d a flight we were usually able to scrape up enough money to eat and buy enough petrol to fly home.

But I remember one occasion when we were stuck in a country town without any petrol and only enough cash to buy some chops, some potatoes and an onion to make a stew in a kerosene tin, then sleep under the wing of the aircraft. A few curious people came along to see what was going on and luckily we were able to get them to part with 2s 6d for joy flights, and finally we had enough cash to buy petrol and fly back to Sydney.

No industrial awards in those days. We had to work to eat. It was either a matter of keeping the aircraft airborne or there was no money and that was it.'

Goya Henry, aged twelve, wearing his medal

Henry Goya Henry

His name was a puzzle, so was his personality, yet in his day, Henry Goya Henry—or Goya Henry, for short—was the most publicised and controversial air pilot in Australia, and the darling of the Australian press which dubbed him 'Australian Aviation's Bad Boy'.

Born in Grafton in 1901, he seemed destined to attract publicity from his earliest years; his first exploit when he dived into the Clarence River, fully clothed to save a schoolmate from drowning. Goya was just six years old!

It won him headlines and there were more when he was presented with the Royal Humane Society's silver medal for bravery. He was its youngest recipient.

Less worthy—and more foolhardy perhaps—was an episode during his early teens when he rode a bicycle along the top of the girders on a local bridge. They were only eighteen inches wide, and the slightest miscalculation would have meant a long drop into the Orara River below. He topped that performance soon afterwards by walking around the narrow rim of a water-tower sixty feet above the ground, and was severely censured when he rowed a boat which he had made from roofing iron, from Yamba beach over the bar and back into an estuary.

Nothing seemed to stop young Goya. At the age of fourteen, he shipped aboard an interstate vessel as an ordinary seaman, got an honourable discharge later and used it to join the crew of a seven-masted barquentine and sailed to America and back.

In 1928, his first disappointment: he was narrowly beaten by his brother Ernest in selection for the Olympic Games. However he did well, was one of the first Australian swimmers to break the minute for 100 yards.

(Today, at the age of eighty-seven, when brother Ernest, Australia's oldest living Olympic medallist, is asked for an opinion on his late brother, shakes his head, sighs and says, 'He was irascible'.)

It's not surprising then, that in 1928 he decided on a flying career. The element of danger suited him exactly and he got his wings the same year. It marked the beginning of a remarkable career in the air—and on the ground—unequalled by any other Australian aviator. To say he left his mark on Australian aviation would be an understatement; he turned it around, took on the federal government and was responsible for a complete overhaul of flying regulations which applied then to the aviation industry.

It's hard not to talk in superlatives when discussing Goya Henry and his turbulent ways. He was the first man to fly under Sydney Harbour bridge (and later the Clarence River bridge at Grafton) in 1932, and although regarded as a fine pilot and flying instructor he was involved in no less than twenty-four forced landings in a variety of locations during more than twenty years as a commercial pilot.

Taking off from Bong Bong racecourse near Bowral, New South Wales with one passenger in a Gypsy Moth in 1929, the plane developed engine trouble and failed to rise. It hit high tension wires, the wings burst into flame and the plane dropped to the ground and rolled over a few times. Miraculously, neither man was hurt and when rescuers arrived they found Goya poking around in the debris looking for spare parts.

Despite his frequent appearances in the newspapers, he was not a publicity hunter. Indeed, he was something of a loner, reticent about his feelings and not inclined to make friends easily. The son of a doctor and with brothers also professionals (one was an MLA) Goya was the family's 'odd lot' and is remembered today for his colourful deeds rather than himself by those, still living, who remember him.

Nancy Bird-Walton, well-known pioneer aviatrix and author, says that 'he was a gentleman', and remembers him as a skilled flier impatient with regulations and who, instead of circling Mascot aerodrome in one direction as the regulations required, invariably flew the other way. He didn't like taxiing and instead of moving slowly across the tarmac and on to the strip, often revved up inside the hangar and flew straight out and into the air. Naturally, these infractions did not go unnoticed by the Civil Aviation Department which, finally, would mount a determined campaign against him.

As a broadcaster I had followed the career of Goya Henry for some time and wanted to meet and interview him. It was during the 1960s and his flying days were behind him, but with his neat moustache and clipped British accent a comparison with the fictional character Biggles was inescapable. I asked him to tell me something about his flying career.

'I soloed in June 1928, and after that I flew regularly until the late 1950s. According to my log book, the total hours were slightly less than 8000 although I flew considerably more than that because I doctored entries to spin out the required time between overhauls which were expensive.

No pilot ever forgets his solo . . . his first flight alone. I was frightened out of my life . . . my knees were wobbling at take-off, but I made a reasonable circuit of the field and landed to the satisfaction of my instructor, Travis Shortridge. My feeling of satisfaction when I landed though was equalled by dismay when Shortridge said, "That was good. Now go round and do it again!"

I realised later that there was sound psychology behind his advice. After doing it once I might have thought I had fluked it.

As a commercial pilot I eventually flew many types . . . thirty-eight, according to my log book. Of course in the 1920s and 1930s there were not as many restrictions on fliers as there are today. If you wanted to do some flying in the moonlight, you'd do it. No nonsense then about aerodrome lights or getting permission. We used car headlights for take-offs and landings.'

In answer to a question, Goya looked at his boots and muttered,

'Yes, I flew under Sydney Harbour bridge. I was the first pilot to do it but it wasn't anything to be proud of. Any man who couldn't have done it with one hand tied behind his back wasn't fit to fly. The clearance in the middle at mean high tide was 172 feet 6 inches.'

It seemed a reasonable thing to do, the way he put it. One could hear him explaining it in court and expecting to be let off with a caution.

'I've had dozens of forced landings, all in the suburbs of Sydney, because engines were not so reliable in my early days as now. For instance, on Manly golf links . . . on number one fairway outside the clubhouse. I chose the spot well. I was invited in and they bought me a beer. No damage to the plane. Another spot was at Earlwood, also at Botany and at Long Beach . . . again on golf links and yet again in a spinach patch near Mascot aerodrome.

In the 1920s of course, flying was considered a hazardous and adventurous occupation, but it didn't detract from the fun.

My worst experience was one violent day in 1930. I took off from Mascot bound for Brisbane in foul weather. I was at fault; I shouldn't have gone but I'd been waiting four days for better conditions and got sick of it and set off. The aircraft was a German Junkers monoplane. It had two seats . . . in this case, one for me and the other for a passenger.

We made it to the Hawkesbury where the weather progressively worsened and I was bumping my head on the clouds as they say, with a ceiling of about four hundred feet, so I decided to return to Mascot. However, the combination of a sick engine and too much cargo on board started to tell. I could hardly maintain height, then sudden engine failure during a tight turn and I was too low to recover.

I hit the rocks at Fairlight near Manly. Luckily, the plane didn't hit the water because it would have sunk immediately. In the impact the passenger was killed instantly. I was fortunate enough to survive. I lost the lower part of a leg.

It didn't keep me out of the air for long, though . . . only about four months. I soon got used to a cork-and-aluminium artificial leg.

The authorities objected strongly to me wanting to fly again, in fact forbade me to do so, but unknown to them I did my first solo after the accident without any trouble. It was at night . . . the only illumination for take-off and landing being the headlights of a friend's car.

I ignored the demands of the Civil Aviation Department and resumed my flying career. Soon afterwards I was flying a woman passenger north when I had an unfortunate forced landing at Wyong. The passenger, although shaken was unhurt, but with the impact my artificial leg went right through the side of the fuselage. The lady had already scrambled free and I had to ask her to turn her back so that I could take my pants off and unstrap the leg.

After that Civil Aviation gave up on me and I flew another 7000 hours as a commercial pilot with an artificial leg before I retired.'

He said it without the blink of an eye, making it sound like a perfectly normal thing to do.

Whether it was due to modesty or not, he had leapfrogged the most spectacular episode of an already remarkable career and one which took place, not in the air but finally in the high courts of Australia.

Goya Henry in later years

The legal battle began soon after the Civil Aviation Department, which had had Goya in its sights for years, suspended his flying license for fourteen days following a minor infringement. He ignored it and continued to fly. The Department suspended his license indefinitely and fined him £2. He refused to pay and took the Department to court, maintaining that the Commonwealth had no powers to control flying or fliers within any one state of Australia. It was a surprise, and from the beginning attracted attention in legal circles. Goya briefed Clive Evatt, QC and the fight in the courts persisted for two years with as many as four QCs on one occasion defending him with the argument that the Civil Aviation Department had no right to suspend his license because it was illegal, nor did it have the right to try a pilot in secret then deprive him of his livelihood without giving him a chance to state his case. It was obvious that he hated bureaucrats.

However, more was involved here than stubbornness or personal pique. It was accepted that Goya Henry believed in regulations as they applied to air safety but not in the nitpicking, high-handed way the Department treated the growing number of pilots in Australia. Goya became their champion.

He lodged appeal after appeal and finally, in 1936 a verdict was delivered by the full bench of the High Court, that the Commonwealth had no general control over civil aviation in Australia, and that the existing regulations, framed in 1920 were invalid. Goya Henry had won and once again he was in the headlines. The Commonwealth tried to maintain the status quo however with a referendum but it was defeated. Finally, chaos was averted by the combined efforts of pilots and airlines in scrupulously observing safety procedures in matters of flying and airworthiness, proving that they could behave responsibly without incessant government interference. It was not surprising that when new regulations were framed, Goya Henry was not granted a licence in spite of his undoubted skills as a pilot and instructor. Yet he continued to fly, and without penalty.

He applied for aircrew with the RAAF during World War II but was rejected. Even in its late stages when standards were relaxed somewhat, it seemed that one-legged pilots were not much in demand, and despite his long courtship with danger in the air, it somehow seemed inappropriate that he should die in retirement, peacefully and in his own bed in 1974 at the age of seventy-three.

Recently, an elderly man named Frank Walters took a bulky parcel to the Mitchell Library in Sydney and handed it in at the front desk. It was Goya Henry's scrapbook and logbooks which he had entrusted to Frank before he died. He had been a friend and admirer for most of his life. Frank says:

'When I was eighteen I went to work for Goya at Mascot aerodrome. At the time he was providing joy-rides for ten shillings a head in a two-place Genairco biplane. It was called the *Jolly Roger* and one of its features was that when it was on the ground, the pilot couldn't see where he was going, because of the shape of the fuselage. One of my jobs was to run alongside the plane with one hand on the wingtip when Goya was taxiing and at the right time drag on it, swinging the plane round into the right position for take-off.

Well, one morning a Fox Moth carrying passengers from Bega burst a tyre on landing. No damage was done and nobody was hurt but the empty plane was left at the side of the strip awaiting a new tyre.

I saw it as Goya taxied out, but didn't know it was stationary. I thought it was taxiing away from us, so instead of guiding him around the Moth I let him go on and he taxied right into it. There was a terrible crash as Goya's prop chewed into the other plane and soon they were locked together. Both were badly damaged and I knew that repairs would cost tens of thousands of pounds.

I tell you, it was by far the worst, the most terrible thing that ever happened to me—before or since. I stood there terrified, then Goya climbed out of what was left of his Glenairco and came over to me. I turned and was about to run back to the hangar to get my things, climb on my pushbike and clear out for good, but Goya said, "Where do you think you're going?"

"Home," I said. "I'm finished. It was all my fault."

"You're not going anywhere," he said, looking hard at me. "You made a mistake and having made it, I know you won't make it again. If I go and employ somebody else he might make the same mistake with the same result." '

No wonder Frank liked the man.

G.U. Allen

Today, at the age of ninety-one he sits quietly in an easy chair at his home in Palm Beach, Sydney. His record: forty-four years as a pilot, with 70 000 hours in the air flying all kinds of aeroplanes—421 different types altogether—many of them in the kinds of weather which would daunt pilots today. He was co-pilot with Charles Kingsford Smith on many of his record-breaking flights and no history of Australian aviation would be complete without him.

Souvenirs, photographs, maps, trivia and other reminders of his adventurous past lie on a table in front of him . . . at his side, a slim briefcase, containing several logbooks with handwritten details of every flight he ever made, is available for easy reference. On the wall opposite, a portrait by William Dobell; as if mocking the passing of the years it shows 'Scotty' Allen as a much younger man.

He was in the Royal Flying Corps in England and was just seventeen when he made his first solo flight in 1918 in an Avro 504K biplane. After World War I he enlisted with the Royal Air Force (RAF) and flew many types of aircraft on service in Egypt, India and the Sudan.

Returning to England in 1930, he saw an advertisement in a newspaper. It stated that two representatives of the newly-formed Australian National Airlines (ANA), Charles Kingsford Smith and Charles Ulm were in Britain looking for pilots to fly their planes in Australia and were inviting applications for the jobs:

'I knew I couldn't leave the RAF for another three years but I applied just for fun. Soon afterwards I got a reply asking me to go to London for an interview. I met Smith and Ulm and told them about my situation, but they interviewed me just the same and three weeks later, to my great surprise I was told that my release from the RAF

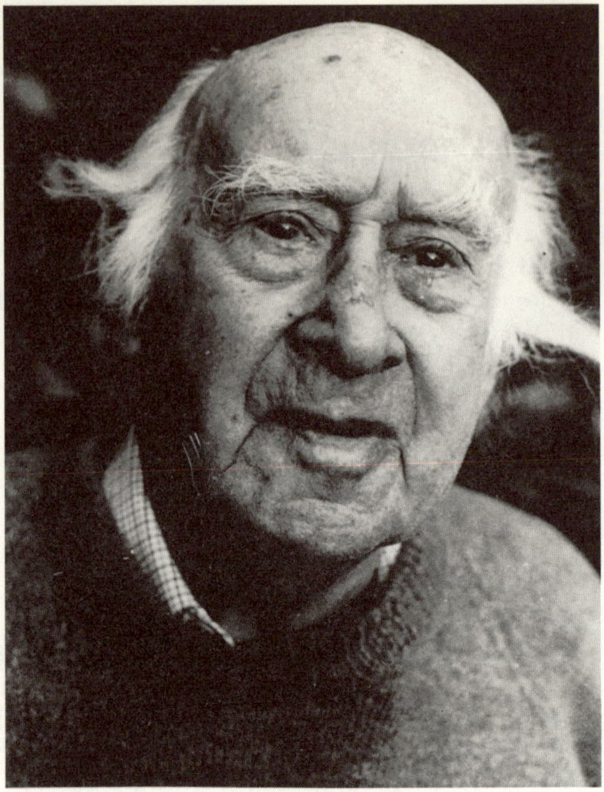

'Scotty' Allen today

had been arranged through the Director of Civil Aviation, and soon after that I was sailing on *Esperance Bay* bound for Sydney.

The day I arrived Ulm met me, took me straight to Mascot and showed me a big monoplane sitting on the tarmac. It had three Pratt and Whitney engines, was fabric-covered and although Fokker-designed was built by Avro in England, hence its name: Avro 10. It had seats for two pilots and eight passengers.

Ulm told me all this then asked, "Do you think you can fly it?"

I said, "Let's have a look." I got in, looked over the instruments then got out and asked Ulm one question: "What's its stalling speed?"

"Sixty-five miles an hour."

I said, "All right. Now?"

Ulm nodded. I was about to get on board but he didn't follow me . . . said he was sending an engineer instead.

I asked why. "In case you bend it," he said with a grin.

Well, I started up, took off, flew the big plane around for a while and found it to be very comfortable. The only navigational aids were a compass, an altimeter and a turn-and-bank indicator but I flew Avro 10's for ANA for three years after that and in all weathers. I flew the first commercial flight from Sydney to Melbourne in 1930. The flight

Avro 10 pilots, Kingsford Smith, 'Scotty' Allen and James Mollison

took five hours and twenty-five minutes. I had ten passengers on board, two more than usual, the wind was southwest in my teeth and we never saw the ground once, at least not until we were on the outskirts of Melbourne and I knew we were over flat country. I had plotted a course to the right of the true course so that if I spotted a main road or railway line I would know in which direction to turn in order to find Essendon aerodrome.

I brought the plane down until we were flying at fifty or sixty feet above the ground at a speed of 95 miles an hour and luck was with us. I spotted a railway station and just had time to read the name. I wrote a note and passed it to my second pilot, Pat Hall. When he read "Sunshine" he burst out laughing. We hadn't seen any so far. Soon afterwards I spotted the hangars and we landed at Essendon alongside the reservoir.

The next day we returned to Sydney with another full plane and the weather was no better; another long trip and we had flown blind from Sydney to Melbourne and back again.

ANA owned five Avro 10s which were flown between Australia's capital cities by Smithy, myself and other pilots who were well known at the time: James Mollison, Paddy Sheppard, Travis Shortridge, Pat Hall, and others.'

The planes had romantic names: *Southern Moon, Southern Cross, Southern Sky, Southern Sun* and *Southern Cloud.* Tragedy hit ANA when

Cloud, piloted by Travis Shortridge and a trainee pilot, Charles Dunnell disappeared one stormy Saturday in 1931 on a flight from Sydney to Melbourne. Despite a wide search over rugged country in Victoria and New South Wales with Scotty and the other ANA pilots flying their Avro 10s at treetop level and ground parties out everywhere, the plane wreckage and the remains of its passengers and crew were not found until twenty-seven years later, in 1958 when a carpenter, employed by the Snowy Mountain Authority in southern New South Wales stumbled over them in the bush on his day off.

It was Australia's first commercial airline disaster. As a result of the tragedy, Australian National Airlines folded, but not before the management had presented Kingsford Smith with *Southern Cross* in appreciation of his part in forming the company. Scotty Allen was his co-pilot on many of his record-breaking flights which followed.

Together they were the first pilots to fly the mail from Australia to England in 1931. They did the same to Bangladesh in the same year. Scotty flew the first commercial flight from the mainland of Australia to Tasmania also in that year.

Allen remembers an interesting forced landing in *Southern Cross* which illustrates the casual attitudes of not only pilots but passengers to mishaps in the early 1930s.

'It was on a domestic flight from Melbourne to Launceston. We hadn't been in the air long when an oil line broke and oil spattered everywhere. I looked at my map in a hurry and noted that there was an emergency landing strip on the extreme tip of Wilson's Promontory in southern Victoria. I found it all right and put the plane down without mishap.

My second pilot, Ernie Aldis, the passengers and myself got out and looked around. The strip was deserted but there was a small shed nearby with emergency fuel and oil supplies inside. It was locked. I was the smallest person in the group so some of the passengers gave me a leg up. I broke the window, got in, retrieved some oil, then went back to the plane, repaired the line, filled her up with oil, everybody got back on board and we resumed our flight to Tassie.

Just the other day, I got a letter from one of the passengers on that flight. He had taken photos of the event and sent me some copies.'

It's a matter for regret that once history has made its mark, it leaves little behind. All too soon, it seems, yesterday is swamped by today, pushed along by the young, eager to make history of their own, and left behind high and dry, far removed from heroic events and the cheers of the crowd, a few pitiful scraps of what was.

I was reminded of it one day in the early 1950s when I was mooning

'Scotty' Allen with 'roadside' repairs (Wilson's Promontory, 1930)

about in a Sydney museum. Among a heap of miscellaneous exhibits I came across a big barnacle-encrusted rubber tyre, more than a metre across with 'Silvertown Goodrich' impressed in it; it was around a wheel and some bits of twisted metal.

It was all that was left of the proud saga of Sir Charles Kingsford Smith, part of the undercarriage of his Lockheed Altair dredged up by fishermen working in the Bay of Bengal.

I knew the details but Ian Debenham, an assistant curator at the museum added more. He said, 'Smithy' bought the plane in 1934 and flew with P.G. Taylor in it to America. It was the first time such a flight across the Pacific had been made. 'Smithy' had wanted to compete with the plane in the MacRobertson Air Race but had had trouble with the aircraft and hadn't been able to make it, much to the disapproval of the Australian public who felt that if he had entered, he would have won.

'That was what goaded him into his last record-breaking attempt from London in November, 1935. Seventy hours out of London all contact with him was lost and it's believed he became disoriented, let down his undercarriage over an island in the Bay of Bengal, hit the treetops and crashed in the sea beyond. There is no doubt about the identity of the wreckage; specialists from the Lockheed Company identified it from serial numbers stamped on the parts.'

It reminded me of another scrap of history which came to light when 'Scotty' Allen was sifting through his memorabilia on my behalf and came across a crumpled piece of paper.

He explained that the engines of the Avro 10 were so close to the cockpit that talking, even yelling by pilots at each other was useless and the only possible means of communication was by handwritten notes. This was one of them, written by Kingsford Smith to 'Scotty' somewhere over the Indian Ocean between Karachi and Calcutta while carrying the first airmail from England to Australia in 1930.

Bearing in mind that hundreds of such notes—many of historical importance—must have been passed between the two during their working lives, it's a pity that this one was so banal. It read:

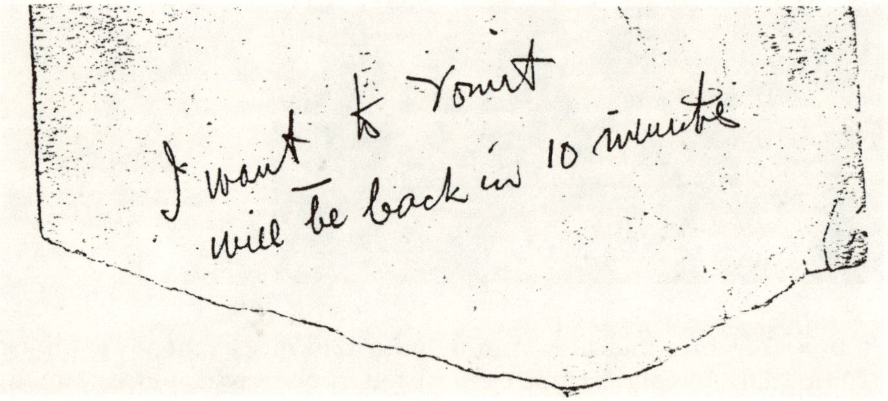

Shops and shopgirls

Working conditions in Australia today with penalty rates, 'sickies', flexitime, maternity leave, shorter working hours and a host of other benefits deemed necessary for the health and well-being of the workers make working a breeze compared with the lot of the workforce in the 1930s.

There was only one course for working men and women to follow: get a job and hold it, do as one was told and no questions asked.

While unions today try hard to provide a utopia for workers, the bosses, during the depressed 1930s had already found theirs: a compliant workforce and an employers' market.

Veronica West, an employee at the time says:

'In 1915 I got my first job as a junior shop assistant at David Jones's store in Sydney. Life wasn't easy for shop assistants then. We worked nine hours a day and the pay was £2 14s 6d per week for seniors and 12s 6d for juniors. We had to wear black frocks and stand up all day, because there was nowhere to sit down behind the counters in the departments, but sometimes we could sneak away for a short time into a fitting room for a sit down. We changed from our black frocks into our street clothes to go home.

In 1912, when I was twenty, permanent waves were introduced into Australia and I was one of the lucky ones chosen by the firm to have my hair done in a demonstration for account customers, who were considered to be very important people then. I sat for four hours to have my hair curled. It was straight to start with but by the time it was over it was curly and very, very frizzy.

I also remember when silk stockings were introduced into Australia. At first, the silk only went down as far as the ankle or a little above and then there was cotton the rest of the way. Later it went from the toe to the knee and finally they were all silk. They cost 25 shillings a pair, and only wealthy women could afford to buy them.'

A decade later, in 1934, working conditions for drapery store employees in Melbourne were no better than they had been when Veronica West started work in Sydney. The Myer Emporium dominated Bourke Street where many other drapers were centred. Buckley and Nunn was next door, The Leviathan and London Stores were over the road and a short distance away, Foy and Gibson, Mantons and Treadways.

Milveh Dorman, then aged sixteen and a 'shopgirl' was selling merchandise in the glove department at Treadways. Looking back, she says:

'I started there in 1932 when I was just fourteen. The Depression was on and I was lucky to get a job. I worked at Treadways for nine years. Apart from late shopping on Friday nights, we worked from nine till six each weekday with half an hour for lunch and on Saturdays from 9 am till 1 pm.

We wore black frocks which we bought ourselves, and were expected to wear hats to work. I was so poor, I remember I wore the same dress to work every day for six months, washing it at night and hoping it would be dry by next morning.

I lived at Sandringham, half an hour's train ride from the city and I think the hardest thing for me was arriving home at about eleven on a Friday night, dog tired and with swollen ankles, knowing that I had to get up again next morning and be at Treadways ready to start again at nine.

We weren't allowed to sit down, you see, not even when we had our "pain" and standing from nine on a Friday morning until nine at night, with half hours off for meals was very hard. The only chairs available were on the other side of the counter for the convenience of customers. We couldn't complain to the higher-ups when we weren't well, because they were all men. Girls wouldn't dream of mentioning such things to men.

There wasn't much future in the job. A girl had no prospects because it was assumed she would leave and get married within a few years. Serving behind a counter was the thing lots of girls did—it was a step above working in a factory—and like every other girl I accepted it.

The wages? I can't remember but they were very low. The girls were expected to take so much in sales every week. If we fell behind too often we were in danger of getting the sack.

Customers wanting gloves were given the kind of service they

Milveh Dorman, aged fifteen, in her black dress

might not get now. Small cushions were provided on the counter, the customers would rest their elbows on them while the assistants fitted each glove, finger by finger and we were most polite, even servile. Some customers expected to be addressed as "Madam".

Each floor at Treadways had a floorwalker who was well-dressed and kept an eye on things. He was an important member of the staff and had to be watched; he cut an impressive figure as he strode about the shop. If the hosiery department—next to ours—had customers waiting and we were slack we had to serve there, too. He would call, "Forward, Miss Dorman" in my case, or if there was a dispute about one of my sales dockets he would call, "Forward, 159!" (That was my number.)

Assistants didn't handle change. When a purchase was made, the money and docket were put into a spring-loaded container, the top was screwed on and with a pull on a handle it was catapulted along overhead wires to a cashier in a box above the floor of each

An Australian city store glove department prior to World War I

department. She returned the change and cancelled docket to the assistant who handed both to the customer.

From time to time Treadways hired private detectives to try and catch employees who were believed to be stealing money, but we always guessed who they were because they would give the correct money for purchases, then leave in a hurry without waiting for sales dockets. Actually, there wasn't much theft by the staff. In those days people held on to their jobs like grim death, because if they got sacked and left without a reference it would be almost impossible for them to get one anywhere else.

We were a close-knit bunch in the glove department. We knew a lot about our boss, Miss T., and she knew a lot about us, and gossip was rife.

There was surprise all round one day when one of the girls, Grace, said she was leaving because she was ill, but begged Miss T. to hold her job open until she felt better and returned. The boss agreed but after some weeks became suspicious and asked us if we knew what was going on. We didn't. Some months passed without a word from Grace, then one day, a fellow-employee Peggy and I met one of Grace's so-called friends in the street. She told us "in confidence", of course that Grace had got herself into trouble, had had "an illegal operation", had nearly died and was still getting over it. She was terrified that her job might not still be available if Miss T. found out.

Peggy and I kept the information to ourselves, but eventually Miss T. found out from another source, also that Peggy and I had kept it from her. There was much friction after that, so Peggy and I had a talk with a glove salesman who also owned a glove-making factory in Melbourne and he offered us jobs making them instead of selling them. We accepted.

We left quietly after six one paynight in 1941, without a goodbye from anyone, unlike the frequent brides-to-be who, on each occasion were accorded a little ceremony of farewell, when the staff manager would come down from the office, congratulate the lass and on behalf of Treadways present her with a small gift to put in her glory box.

We didn't mind missing out. In the glove factory we could sit down all day, sick or well and importantly, without working on Friday nights or Saturday mornings. When we had learned how to sew gloves—it didn't take long—the wages were much better, too.

Looking back now on my decision to leave Treadways, I realise what a risk I took. My parents had moved interstate. As a single girl I lived alone in a room in the city, and had my job at the glove factory not worked out and I had been sacked I would have found it hard to find another at short notice.

Luckily, everything was fine. A power machine was not hard to use and when I took time off to get married later, my fellow-machinists presented me with a Royal Doulton vase. I still have it and prize it highly.'

Young Griffo, boxer

If Ray Mitchell, aged seventy-two, tells you that back in the 1890s a bare-knuckle fighter nicknamed 'Young Griffo' was the world's best, you'd better listen because Ray was not only once a welterweight boxer himself, but he is known far and wide as 'Mr Boxing' and was awarded an MBE in 1972 for his contribution to 'boxing and sporting journalism'. He is an authority on the noble art and can name any boxer of worth who fought in the Australian ring—or elsewhere—from the days of the First Fleet.

'When I was a kid my parents were interested in boxing, so were relatives who lived next door. They were always talking about Young Griffo's exploits and I think I got to know more about him than some of my own family. He was certainly the most successful bare-knuckle fighter of his day.

He was a brilliant boxer but he loved to drink, and his trainers often locked him up for a few days before a fight so that he would be sober in the ring. They did that on 2 September 1890, yet just two days before his fight against "Torpedo" Billy Murphy for the title of World Featherweight, he escaped and was seen by a newspaperman in a Port Jackson pub in Sydney, "gorging himself on potatoes in their jackets, washed down with draughts of beer". It made no difference . . . he won the fight and the title.

Six months later he defended his world title against Queenslander, George Powell in Sydney. He began training at Bondi but gave it away after a week and went back to drinking. There was another

Ray Mitchell, sports journalist (left) being interviewed on ABC radio

story in the papers about him taking a girl in a bashed-up bustle for frequent walks in the Domain at night. Certainly it wasn't the right sort of training for a title fight, but it made no difference. Young Griffo had no trouble with Powell. In fact, he was so much in control of the fight that during the fifteenth round he stopped fighting, pointed to the canvas and said to Powell, "Look, there's a shilling!" In the nineteenth he stopped to blow his nose and Powell, who was a long way behind on points dashed in and hit him. It made the champion angry and he floored Powell twice. In fact, by round twenty Powell was getting such a beating that he sat down on the canvas, completely demoralised. The ref. disqualified him immediately and crowned Griffo the winner.'

Ray says that 'Griffo' was born Alfred Griffiths in 1871 in Bendigo, Victoria. As a child he sold newspapers and from the age of fifteen fought in bare-knuckle fights. He won the Newsboy Championships in 1887. By the time he was twenty he had totted up an impressive string of wins in Australia and was looked on as being unbeatable. He was world champion by the time he was nineteen and there were plenty of contenders for the crown. One of them, Jim Barron fought him at Darlinghurst in 1893. They drew after 22 rounds; Young Griffo retained his lightweight title and Barron told him he should try his luck in America.

He agreed, got himself booked on a ship called *Alameda* but was blind drunk the day it sailed and missed it. Another berth was booked

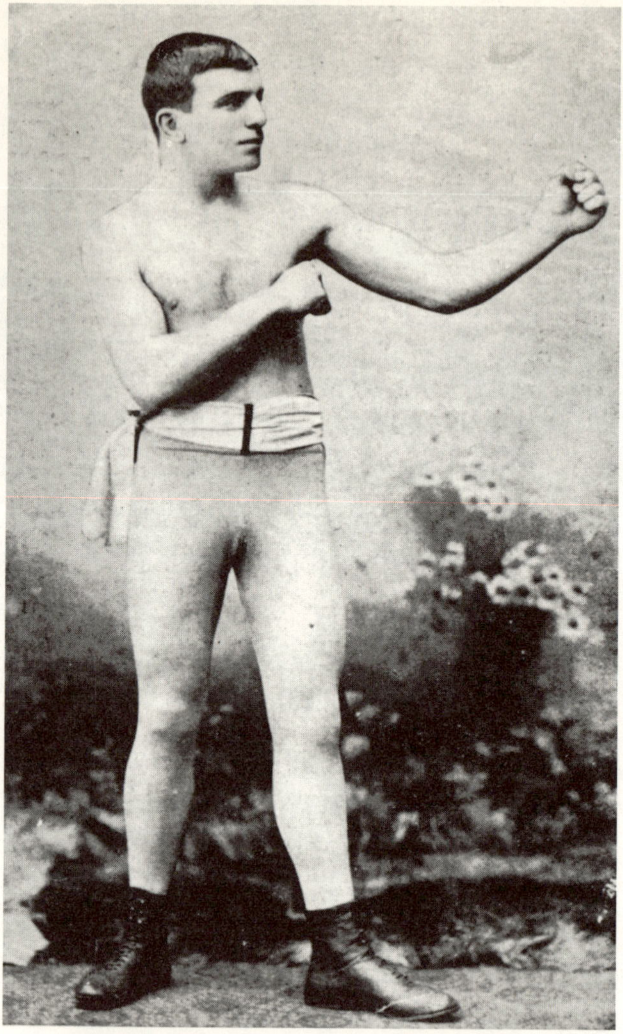

Young Griffo as a young man

for him on *Mariposa.* Griffo went on board and his friends lined the shore ready to wave him goodbye, but as the ship began to move, he panicked and leapt from the ship to the wharf. Later, when *Alameda* returned to Sydney, an American boxer's agent tried again and was successful. Griffo went on board, stayed there, sailed to America and never saw Australia again.

He had his first fight in Chicago in November 1893, when he beat his opponent, 'Young Scotty', an African-American welterweight in six rounds, and many other successful bouts followed. In 1894 Griffo fought Jack McAuliffe, the World Lightweight champion in New York. (McAuliffe, according to the record books is one of the few undefeated world champions.) When the bell rang at the end of the fight

McAuliffe said,'You won that, Griff' but the referee crowned McAuliffe the winner on points! Ray reports:

'The fans nearly tore the place down! The story was that the ref., Maxie Moore had kept the score with marbles in his pockets and he got his pockets mixed up!

It was Griffo's first defeat in 167 fights! His slide downwards started soon afterwards. In 1896 he was sent to jail for six months for disturbing the peace. He served his term and returned to boxing but without much success. In 1899 he was arrested again for the same offence, was found to be suffering from the DTs and was committed to a detention hospital. Yet he recovered, went back to the ring in 1900 and retired in 1904 when he was thirty-three.

Later, surprisingly, he became a teetotaller, befriended a boxer called Collins and when the latter died, his widow allowed Griffo to live at her boarding house in New York rent free.

During the last years of his life he could be found every day sitting on a step in 42nd Street. Admirers gave him money and several took up a collection so that he could return to Australia. He wouldn't have it. He said, "What's the use of me going home? Me old man wouldn't recognise me now."

One day he wasn't there. He was found in his bed, dead at the age of fifty-six. The year was 1927.

Griffo was the greatest. Mighty in the ring, and outside it—when he was sober—a big, peaceful man. He was fond of performing tricks in bars. He'd stand on a handkerchief and say, "I challenge anybody to hit me in the kisser without me moving me feet." Nobody could, and despite his big fight-hardened hands he could pluck a fly from the air, let it go then catch it again between thumb and forefinger. His favourite stunt was to borrow a pocket watch, hang it on a wall, stand back and throw a straight left at it, breaking the glass but leaving the rest of the watch undamaged.

In 1989 I went to New York with an ex-boxer friend, Jack Stitt, in search of his grave. We found it in Woodlawn Cemetery. The small headstone was covered with weeds. I cleared them away and read the inscription. There were a couple of errors in the spelling and the date but it read, "Young Griffo . . . Alfred Griffith, 1880–1927. Erected by his Australian friends."

He wasn't the first Australian champion to die in America. First, there was Les Darcy in 1917 then Griffo in 1927 and Phar Lap in 1932.'

John Olsen's Museum

In the 1950s when the postmaster general's department was responsible not only for our mail but for our telephone system, there was a wonderful museum on the first floor of a building in Pitt Street, Sydney. Known as the Post Office Museum it was maintained largely by the enthusiasm of its curator, John Olsen. He had a way of bringing the past close to the present as he walked around from exhibit to exhibit describing each piece and throwing in an anecdote or two about it.

'People used to say "I'll meet you under the post office clock," and certainly it was a favourite meeting place for Australians everywhere, but few knew that our first post office clock belonged to a man named Isaac Nichols. He was Australia's first postmaster and appointed to the position on 25 April 1809. The clock stood in his home which was also the post office in High Street, Sydney now called lower George Street.'

It was a handsome mantel clock, still working and with a silvery chime.

Next, a portrait of an impressive looking man in a resplendent uniform, a long red coat with gold buttons, and gold lace at the cuffs; a top hat with gold braid and a bow tie.

'A typical postman in the mid-1850s, he was highly thought of and was well-paid: £2 per week. ($4)'

This American-style coach carried mail and passengers in western New South Wales until about 1890. Managed by Morris Brothers, it competed with Cobb and Co., who began a similar service in 1862

Then to a huge dusty book labelled 'Irregularities Book' in copperplate and it recorded fines imposed on post office employees for various offences in the early 1900s. A typical entry revealed that a telegraphist used improper language to another. He was fined one pound, which was about two weeks wages then.

'Many of the mails then were carried on horseback, certainly to the smaller towns, that is until the transport of mails by coach, beginning in New South Wales in 1862. Cobb and Co. began and were followed by other contractors and one of the quaint customs of the time: the coaching horn.'

He showed me one. It was made of copper and measured three feet in length.

'As a coach on a mail run approached a country town the driver blew the horn as a warning that he was nearing the post office. Quite often if a town was small, the coach wouldn't stop at all; the driver would throw the incoming mail off and the postmaster would toss the outgoing mail up to the driver as horses and coach swept past.

Australia had postage stamps before Great Britain. They were introduced on 1 November 1838 with the stamps embossed on the corners of envelopes. They sold at 1s 3d a dozen and were not popular to start with; people liked to use their own envelopes and the

The first section of Sydney GPO, built in 1872 and opened in 1874

The Leyland 'warhorse'. First used by the Postmaster General's Department before World War I, it was still in use in 1943. This photograph was taken in 1937

Sydney suburban letter carriers in 1905. They delivered mail twice a day, and their chances of promotion were good

old system of paying cash for the sending of letters, that is paying twopence each to postmen when delivering them or before they were sent. Stamps were made compulsory in 1852, two years after stick-on stamps came out in denominations of a penny, twopence and threepence. They had views of Sydney on them, based on the design of the great seal of the colony.'

Another photograph (see page 76), of an old delivery truck had a special place among the exhibits.

'It was known as "The warhorse" and was first used to carry mail around Sydney before World War I. When war was declared it went overseas with the troops and carried stores on the battlefields. After the war it returned to Australia and was still in use in 1943 when a casual driver noticed shrapnel marks on the radiator and recognised it as the same truck he had driven while in the Army in France more than twenty-five years before.'

The building of Sydney GPO which began in 1872 was illustrated with some remarkably fine photographs in another part of this unique museum. It was built in three sections . . . first the George Street end (see page 76), then the other end in Pitt Street and finally both were topped by the clock tower. According to John Olsen it cost an enormous amount of money hence the need to build it over a period of twenty-one years.

He said that the custom then—and earlier—to house government departments in substantial, solid buildings even when their importance or location didn't warrant it, was in accordance with an official belief that it was necessary to remind the populace that British administration and British justice, like the buildings were substantial and lasting.

I valued the Post Office Museum and John Olsen's voluminous knowledge of our postal history. However, in 1975 when Telecom assumed control of the Australian domestic telephone system, leaving the postal system to the newly-named Australia Post, the museum was dismantled, packed into boxes, and despite recent enquiries nobody seems quite sure where it is now. I couldn't find out what happened to John Olsen, either.

A matchmaker

I found her one hot summer's day in the 1950s, an elderly woman sitting quietly behind a desk in a dusty office on the first floor of an old building in Oxford Street, Sydney. At her side, curled up on a cushion a large Siamese cat, whose name I learned later was Tricky Two.

Mrs Holt looked rather tired and bowed-down . . . a bit like her office. Yet there seemed little reason for pessimism; on the walls around her and cluttering up the top of her desk were dozens of photographs of smiling couples, young and old, in silver frames. All were smiling . . . smiling . . . not a scowl or a frown anywhere to break the monotony.

Mrs Holt had brought happiness to them all. Like thousands of other hopefuls they had climbed the rickety stairs to her long-established, one-woman matrimonial agency in search of lasting love (or a reasonably accurate facsimile) and thanks to her skills had been successful. First, the introduction, then some nurturing, and with a final nudge from the resourceful Mrs H., a date in a church or registry office and they were launched on the unpredictable seas of matrimony.

Unfortunately, most of the photographs were old; it was obvious that the agency was no longer a thriving business and little more than a repository for the old lady, her cat and her memories . . .

I wanted her to tell me about her work and started with an implied compliment that her agency was still at it. I asked about the kinds of people who came to her for help.

'All kinds of people come in here. The shy, the socially inept, the good-looking, the ugly and all of them yearning for companionship. Many suited here have had their spouses die and they have come back to be suited again . . . some again and again after numerous marriages. And I do more than simply ask for their names and addresses.

There are no instant introductions here! Each applicant has to produce references from two well-known people, each a certificate of health and I have to have a long talk with them about themselves. Then a few days have to pass while I check up on their addresses. And applicants, of course have to prove that they are single.

If everything is all right, I put them into separate rooms for a while, then I bring them together and introduce them. I stay with them for a minute or two and talk to break the ice, then I leave them together to see what will happen. It's all very private and confidential. If all seems to be going well I suggest to the man that he should take the woman out for a cup of coffee or to the pictures. If they're not suited, each comes back and we try again.

In the old days I relied heavily on reports from doctors. I could tell from them which girls were virgins and which were not and you'd be surprised at how many virgins were among them.

Many of the women who come in here are the eldest daughters of large families. Often they are the ones who looked after younger brothers and sisters and bore the brunt of their families' problems, taking responsibility and so on while the others went off, found partners and got married. Left on the shelf, they still can't go out and meet somebody because the parents have grown old and need looking after. The result: they have lost confidence and feel that nobody wants them for themselves. It is very hard for these older daughters with marriage in mind to break into established circles of other men and women and find somebody who will love them.

In the 1920s, of course, there were fewer divorces than there are now. It was considered shameful, and divorced men with children, looking for new wives had special problems. I remember a farmer with ten children who came in here looking for somebody who would be a mother to them and himself. I introduced him to a registered nurse aged twenty-eight. She took him on, married him and they must have been happy because they had four children of their own, making fourteen altogether.

In the old days people who found their partners through me used to bring their first babies in . . . but not so much now.

Twenty years ago all young girls had high hopes; they started putting their glory boxes or hope chests together when they were as young as fifteen or sixteen, but if a girl was unmarried at twenty-five she was likely to be an old maid. However, less was expected of prospective partners then than today. Years ago, a working-class woman was glad if she got a home, but today she expects a car, a decent flat, plenty of outings and all kinds of expensive things.'

Her lips pursed in disapproval and the way she said it, necessities sounded like luxuries, even in 1956. Clearly the world had passed her by.

Oxford Street and Mrs Holt's world lost their innocence in the 1970s when liberalism marched in, but oddly, one of Mrs Holt's most straitlaced requirements for prospective spouses before marriage, namely medical certificates, has greater relevance today than it had then . . .

A Crown prosecutor

There is no picture of Buchanan Francis Fraser Telfer to grace these pages, yet no doubt many former wrongdoers, now in their dotage will remember him. 'Buck' Telfer as he was known to his clerk in the old days was a New South Wales crown prosecutor serving the law in the country courts of the state. His influence on the Northern Rivers Circuit where he prosecuted for many years must have been considerable yet due to his position of responsibility perhaps, he kept apart, was something of a loner, but lived well and liked the job, refusing all offers of better legal appointments in the city. A comparison with TV's 'Rumpole of the Bailey' is irresistible.

'I practised for fifty-one years and in general, the laws of punishment for offenders at the turn of the century were much different from today, and the judgements handed down generally were harsher, because in those days society saw the sentences as a form of punishment and as a deterrent to those who might be tempted to emulate them. Rehabilitation was unknown.

In Sydney, where I practised, judges were tough and so were juries and some crimes, like those on the waterfront about the year 1908 encouraged the toughest sentences.

They were the days of two gangs of blackguards: the Blue Metal Push and the Glebe Island Push. They were hard men and their favourite operation, apart from fighting with each other was garrotting police officers. They would come up quietly behind them, grab them by the throat and twisting their ties or other neck gear would half-strangle them, leaving them close to death on many occasions.

At that time the police were not allowed to carry pistols but the gangs' operations became so frequent a special law had to be passed enabling all police to carry arms.

Whenever offenders were caught they were dealt with most severely. Up until 1908 the lash was part of sentences handed down by learned judges for such vicious assaults, and the general public attitude favoured such punishment. Generally it was administered in conjunction with a prison sentence and was thought to be an effective deterrent. I do remember having a conversation with an old police sergeant at the time. He was one of the officers responsible for the arrest of the notorious Jimmy Governor and he reported to me a talk he had had with a criminal who had had the lash, followed by two years in jail. He told the sergeant on his release, "No more lash for me, Sergeant. I'm finished with that."

The end of the lash in this jurisdiction came in 1908 when Mr J. Carruthers was the premier of New South Wales and learned Judge Docker inflicted a punishment of two years on an offender for breaking and entering and also with "a tag", as we called it, of 24 strokes of the lash. However, the day after the sentence was handed down the *Sydney Morning Herald* published a scathing article denouncing the use of the lash, saying that it was a return to barbarism.

The matter was brought up in Parliament and the following week it was deleted from "the tag" and was not used again.'

Eileen Fitzer, MBE

A few years ago Crocodile Dundee impressed the world with his wild adventures in the Australian outback, yet he was a wimp compared with some of the real-life pioneers who carved a life for themselves in the bush during the last century.

Like Ned Tuckwell. In 1864, when South Australia gained control of the Northern Territory, Ned, a carpenter and shipwright joined a fourteen-man expedition about to establish a settlement in the north.

He had already done his duty at home; left four daughters and a heavily-pregnant wife Eliza behind, and as Barbara James tells it in *No Man's Land* the leaders of the McKinley expedition should have heeded good advice and waited until the rainy season was over before they set out; but they were well-equipped, had forty horses and pressed on with their plans. Before long though, the rains came as predicted and the expedition came to a halt at the flooded East Alligator River.

They couldn't go forward and found it impossible to go back, were marooned and after a time, when their supplies ran out they were forced to kill their horses and eat them, Finally, they became desperate, but in a way even Crocodile Dundee wouldn't have thought of, gathered wood, built the frame of a boat, covered it with the hides of the horses they had slaughtered, and launching themselves on the swollen waters of the East Alligator River were carried finally to safety at a settlement appropriately named Escape Cliffs. According to a newspaper report, Ned had proved of great service to the party in building the boat and navigating the frail craft. 'His knowledge of seamanship played a major part in saving the lives of he and his companions,' the report added.

In 1868, Ned took Eliza and his children to live in Darwin where they put down roots and became established. By now, Eliza had two more children, making seven altogether, of whom only two survived.

Despairing of Ned's heavy drinking, Eliza turned from domesticity to religion, joined a local Wesleyan church and campaigned against the evils of alcohol, which must have been a hopeless cause, bearing in mind the number of determined drinkers then—and now—in that heat-stricken part of Australia.

She became increasingly concerned about the effect the rough life of the Northern Territory was having on her daughters, and when a resident, during an argument told the girls 'Your parents can go to hell and I don't care a damn,' their mother, Eliza, who should have turned the other cheek, took him to court instead where he was fined and cautioned.

I heard about the Tuckwells' colourful past from Eliza's granddaughter, Eileen Fitzer:

'I spent all of my childhood in the Northern Territory. I was born at Darwin in 1902, was one of ten children, only five of whom survived past infancy. I had to walk two miles to school each day, but the schooling was not of a very high standard and I was educated in a slipshod kind of way.

Our neighbours owned cattle stations and everybody had to make their own fun. There were bush-race meetings . . . real picnic meetings—with sports and flat races for the children. The last event of the day at the Adelaide River picnic was always "Chase the Greasy Pig" and the person who caught it kept it as the prize. That was in 1914.

I got a limited secondary education, but in 1928 I went down to Melbourne to train as a nurse. I attended night school, studied midwifery and after four years graduated as a nursing sister. Then I returned to Alice Springs where I was employed by the government to work at the Bungalow, formerly one of the Territory's first telegraph stations, two miles from where Alice Springs is today.

Nursing conditions were very crude. While I was there a trachoma eye epidemic broke out and I was nursing in isolation for two months at Heavitree Gap. By the time it was over I had spent seventeen weeks caring for seventeen patients with only two Aborigine girls to help me and the only people who visited were the doctors and the butcher and baker.

In 1934 the Territory medical officer transferred me to Pine Creek as sister in charge of a small hospital. It was really a casualty station for the treatment of injuries among workers in the three goldmines, or for patching up the miners after fights in the local pub.

I went part of the way to Pine Creek by train and when I got there, Clyde Fenton, known all over the Territory as the flying doctor was waiting for me. He looked very different from what I'd been led to expect, was blue-eyed, bearded and if anybody looked like the Saviour, it was him!'

Born at Warrnambool, Victoria in 1901, Clyde Fenton graduated in medicine at Melbourne University in 1925, went to England but driven by a sense of adventure returned to Australia and headed for the outback. However, the life of a plodding GP was not for him.

He learned to fly, applied for a job with the Royal Flying Doctor Service and was rejected. Then with the help of his mother who bought him a second-hand Gypsy Moth aeroplane got a job as medical officer at Katherine, and on his own initiative started a flying ambulance service which later would become the Northern Territory Aerial Medical Service.

He did all the maintenance on his plane and at first the government, cautious of his activities allowed him only the same mileage allowance as that given to public servants driving their own cars.

Fenton was an adventurous, dedicated one-man band and would fly anywhere, under almost any conditions day or night to tend the sick. He had a number of crash landings and in one of them, which left him scarred for life his plane was destroyed. The government, finally impressed by his work bought him another, then proceeded to extract its cost from his salary!

He had a brusque manner, paid scant attention to what he considered were the pinpricking rules of the Civil Aviation Department and that, combined with a disregard for his personal safety in the face of need was the kind of stuff from which folk heroes are made.

In 1940, he joined the RAAF, became a flying instructor and later, as a squadron leader was in charge of an air force unit. At war's end he became a quarantine officer in Melbourne, retired in 1966 and died in 1982.

Eileen Fitzer went on:

'Soon after I settled in Pine Creek, Doctor Fenton, whose practice covered an unbelievably vast area, flew in in his two-seater Gypsy Moth. It was his custom to call in once a week, unless there was some emergency.

It didn't take me long to learn that he had a devilish sense of humour. When I told him that I had never been in a plane, he bet me six bottles of beer that he could take me up and make me sick! I saw it as a challenge and accepted straight away. He explained that there was no intercom between the passenger seat in front and his seat behind, so every now and then, he said he would tap me on the shoulder to make sure I was all right. If I was okay all I had to do was smile.

Well, I got in, he took off and he threw the little plane all over the sky for thirty minutes, finishing up with a spin from a great height with the engine off. I didn't like it, but I kept on turning and grinning at him and I won the bet!

I got used to flying after that, went on many flights with him and became a jack-of-all-trades; I helped him to tie the plane down if bad weather threatened, kept wild goats away (on one occasion they wanted to eat the wings) and laid down flares when he flew in after dark, usually around midnight.

He was a marvellous doctor, would fly anywhere at any time to treat a patient and when on duty wouldn't let anything interfere with his job, which wasn't always easy. On one occasion, he had to land some distance away from an accident in a mine up at Spring Hill, and before the patient could be brought out, the miners had to cut out all the trees and clear a strip so that he could land his little plane, put the patient in the front seat and fly him to Darwin.

Despite his care with patients and his skill as a doctor, he was quite reckless sometimes. There was one famous occasion which had everybody in the Territory talking. He flew into Darwin one evening and did a power-dive over the open-air picture show. People in the audience said he flew so low over their heads that he blocked off the light between the projector and the screen.

As a result his licence was cancelled by the authorities. It was an awkward situation . . . what would happen if an emergency call came in, everybody wondered.

As it happened, I *did* have an emergency at Pine Creek. Some miners came down to the hospital carrying a patient. They were in such a hurry, they hadn't even taken their mining gear off.

"Quick, Sister!" they said. "Get the flying doctor! You must help this man . . . the big boss said so. He could buy the doctor's plane, you know."

They didn't panic me. I was very dignified and said, "I'll put him into bed and then I will decide whether he needs the flying doctor or not."

Well, the men parked themselves outside on the verandah while I took a look at him. He seemed very agitated and rather shocked. As I put him into pyjamas I noticed he had a terrific scar on his body and I thought he might have had an obstruction of some kind which needed urgent medical treatment. I decided I'd have to get on to the chief medical officer in Darwin, so I contacted local police who rang Darwin for me and I spoke with the officer concerned. He said that only the chief administrator could give Doctor Fenton permission to fly again and that he would have to make an appointment to see him. I said, "What if the patient dies in the meantime?"

That fixed it. He went round and saw the administrator at once as a matter of urgency and permission was given for Doctor Fenton to fly to Pine Creek and attend to the patient.

As it turned out, by the time he arrived in his plane the patient had made a remarkable recovery. In fact, he wasn't sick. It was a put-up job by the miners to get Doctor Fenton back in the air again. It worked and I was fooled completely.'

After two years at Pine Creek, Eileen married a long-time friend, Harry Gibbons whom she described as 'a wild Irishman'. Everybody loved him and he was said to be a good drinking companion but not everybody approved. After the wedding, the newlyweds decided to try their luck at Wauchope, south of Tennant Creek where wolfram had just been discovered. They didn't find any but shared the hard life for eighteen months. Eileen was the only white woman there and her skills as a nursing sister were much in demand.

Then, in 1938 the medical officer in Darwin invited her to act as relieving sister at a leprosarium on an island several miles from Darwin. She accepted, cared for one hundred and twenty lepers for three months and found it satisfying work. In 1939 Harry and Eileen bought themselves a hotel at Adelaide River. Then war came and following the bombing of Pearl Harbor by the Japanese in 1941 and the consequent threat to Australia, it was deemed advisable for both to move south. Harry, who had been ill for some time died in Sydney in 1943.

Eight months later, Eileen, unhappy and restless, still in Sydney, was offered a job as nursing sister at Tipperary cattle station in the Territory. She accepted and couldn't wait to get back.

She hadn't been at Tipperary long before she became involved in a kind of drama not uncommon in Australia's north where uncertain communications, dodgy weather and a small population spread over a vast area can turn minor accidents into major emergencies. This one concerned one of Eileen's friends, Tas Fitzer, a police officer who was in charge of a station at Daly River, twenty miles away.

Unknown to Eileen, Tas was in a critical situation at the River. He had been breaking in a colt when it kicked him in the knee, causing serious injury. He needed urgent medical attention, but his pedal radio was out of action, not unusual in the rainy season. He was aware that even if the flying doctor could be told of his predicament, he couldn't land his plane because of the weather. So Tas, a stubborn man, lay in pain on the verandah of his house for seventeen days, with only his black trackers for company. Finally, when he knew that he was becoming delirious, he wrote a note to Eileen at Tipperary and told his best black tracker, Attawomba to deliver it.

Eileen takes up the story:

Tas Fitzer and tracker Attawomba

'It wasn't easy. The rain hadn't stopped and what with crossing swollen creeks and rivers it took Attawomba a day and a half to cover the twenty miles.When I read Tas's note I realised that he was in a bad way and I told the station manager, Harry Scott who rounded up some Aboriginal helpers, got a truck out and we headed for Daly River. We got bogged time and time again, but each time the Aborigines pulled us out.

We got as far as the copper mines, ten miles down the river then realised that it was impossible to drive any further. It was terribly frustrating. However, what we didn't know was that at about that time a peanut cocky—a farmer who grew peanuts—had called on Tas, seen how ill he was and organised a stretcher party to carry him cross-country to Tipperary!

They set out, carried him a great distance through the rain, through bogs and creeks until, incredibly they met up with us at the copper mines!

I took one look at Tas and realised that he was very ill. We made him comfortable in the truck and got back to Tipperary where he insisted that I should look after him "because I was a nurse". I told him it was beyond me, he should be seen by a doctor so I gave him

The Fitzers at home

some morphine, he was taken to an army hospital on the Adelaide River, then transferred to Darwin. He was operated on, had the knee drained and it took him some months to recover.'

Not surprisingly, Tas's accident brought he and Eileen close together. They were married in April, 1945. He was forty-nine, she forty-three, and they established a home in an isolated spot on the Daly River.

A year later, Eileen suffered a health crisis of her own: severe abdominal pains. Again, the pedal radio, vitally important in the Territory failed to work and this time one of Tas's black trackers had to be sent thirty miles on foot to get help. He got through, a phone call was made to Darwin and the navy boom-vessel *Kangaroo* was despatched to help her. Used in conjunction with a crash launch, it rescued Eileen, took her to Darwin hospital and later to Melbourne where she recovered. The story made headlines in Australian newspapers.

'Later, Tas and I lived at a settlement called Timber Creek. It was one of the most remote police stations in the world. Our nearest neighbours were forty miles on one side, and fifty miles on the other. We were surrounded by huge cattle properties. Tas had begun his career at Timber Creek and he was glad to be there again.

His work involved going out with black trackers in search of murderers and cattle thieves, arresting them and bringing them back for trial. He travelled about three thousand miles a year with his black trackers and fifty horses. They would have to change the horses two or three times a day sometimes because of the heat and the heavy packs.

Time and time again I said goodbye to Tas on our front verandah knowing I might not see him again for some months and that he would be patrolling hundreds of miles away. The most wonderful sight in the world was when he was on his way back; he and the trackers would light a fire many miles away to give me the good news that he would soon be home.

During the war he was very busy, tracking not only wrongdoers and arresting them, but going out in search of airmen who had come down and were lost in the country around Darwin.'

Tas Fitzer died in 1966 and his name has been recorded in the Stockman's Hall of Fame in Longreach. Today Eileen Fitzer, MBE, an immensely cheerful woman lives alone in Darwin. She is ninety years old.

Ouch!

It's an ancient illustration (opposite) and not a pretty one, and no doubt it will cause a shudder among many oldies who remember their painful tussles with dentists in the 1920s and 1930s.

Anybody who lived in Melbourne at the time may recall a dentist's sign on a building at the top of Bourke Street; it was familiar to commuters travelling past on cable trams each day and showed a small boy smiling happily and displaying a gap where one of his top teeth had just been extracted. His comment: 'It didn't hurt a bit!'

It was lucky for the dentist that Consumer Affairs weren't operating then, because as any child of that era knew, it was a downright lie. Extraction of teeth hurt like hell in the 1920s and 1930s. Oil of cloves, methylated spirits on cotton wool held in aching decayed teeth gave temporary relief, but inevitably it meant a dreaded visit to the dentist, to get a dodgy needle (which didn't seem to help much) while Dad or Mum held on to our arms and tried to quell our yells as we saw the forceps for the first time and . . .

Despite these depressing reminders of dentistry as it was for many of us, Sydney Levine, a 77-year-old retired periodontist who is interested in Australian dental history claims conditions weren't bad in those days, but a quick inspection of his smile revealed that he still had all his second teeth, which would seem to lessen the value of his opinion.

But delving into dentistry of the past he came up with some interesting facts and a picture or two, one of them proving that the

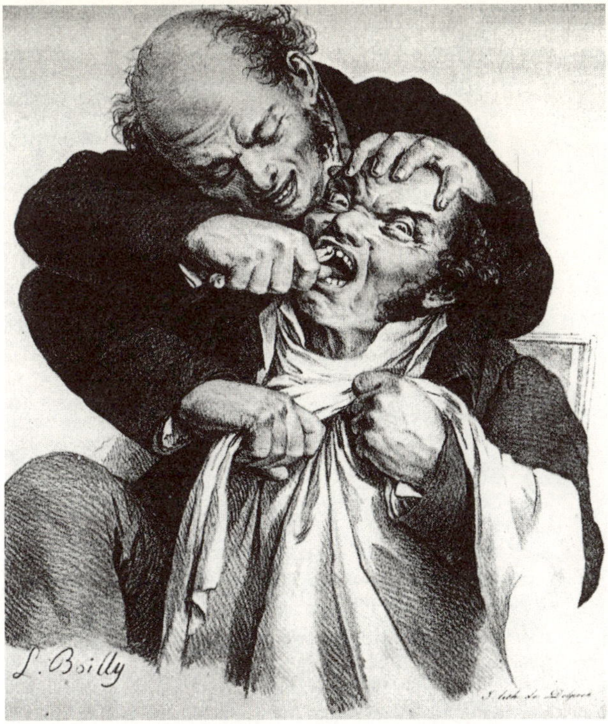

A painful tussle with a dentist

Bourke Street dentist with his fulsome claim that 'it didn't hurt a bit' was not the first of his kind.

Dr Tunnock's Dental Parlor

This self-styled 'doctor' (Dr Tunnock, page 93) in his frockcoat and top hat, with doubtful letters after his name, boasted on the window of his dental parlour that he was 'under the distinguished patronage of His Excellency The Earl of Hopetoun' the first governor of the Commonwealth. True or false, it dates the picture as having been taken about 1902. A flamboyant practitioner, Tunnock also conducted a college for would-be dentists.

The first-known dental notice to appear in an Australian newspaper was published in the *Sydney Gazette* in 1814, suggesting perhaps that patients could save time by having their teeth and feet attended to during the same visit:

JOSEPH HYAMS, Dentist, 31, Pitt-street, respectfully offers his Services to the Public in the Line of his Profession—Scaling, cleaning, and drawing the Tooth, when necessary, without causing pain; and supplying the vacancy with others of pure Ivory.—Also, Corns extracted with ease and safety.—Attendance at home or abroad; and Charges very moderate.

In 1842, J. Emanuel went to great pains to list his skills as a dentist in the columns of the *Australian.* It would be uncharitable perhaps to claim that he exaggerated; sufficient to say that even then, self-praise was no recommendation.

TEETH.—A NEW DISCOVERY!

MR J. EMANUEL, Surgeon-Dentist, begs to submit to the public his peculiar method of supplying artificial and natural teeth, from one to a complete set, upon the beautiful system of self-adhesion, without the aid of springs, wires, clasps, or fastenings of any kind—and above all, are firmer in the mouth—and fixed with that attention to nature so as to excite surprise in the most sceptical. They are so contrived as to adapt themselves to the most tender gums, or remaining stumps, without causing the least pain, rendering the operation of extracting quite unnecessary. They are guaranteed to answer every purpose of articulation and mastication. Mr. E. begs to invite the public to an inspection of the specimens of his effective system of dental mechanism in all its varieties—so free from pain in their application—and which may be seen at his residence daily.

LIST OF CHARGES.

A single tooth	£2 2 0
Stopping with gold cement....	0 10 6
Ditto with pure gold leaf......	0 15 0
Scaling	0 10 6
Extracting...........	0 5 0

In conclusion, Mr. Emanuel wishes to draw the special attention of his patrons to the fact of his being A REGULARLY QUALIFIED SURGEON DENTIST, OF LEYDON COLLEGE, from which institution he obtained his diploma in 1836 to practice in the above art. Since that period he has rendered himself intimately conversant in the various modern improvements in the surgical and mechanical branches of his profession in London, Paris, and other towns on the Continent.

At home from 10, A. M., till 5, P. M.

Residence—Wyatt's Buildings, Castlereagh-street, North.

The following, published in a Sydney directory in 1855 seems a bit over the top.

DENTAL SURGERY IN ALL ITS BRANCHES.

Beautiful Artificial Teeth.

DR. WILSON,

SURGEON DENTIST,

SUPPLIES Beautiful Incorrodible Artificial TEETH of the best Workmanship, and on an entirely new principle, and they so closely resemble the

NATURAL TEETH

as to be readily mistaken for them by the most critical observer.

TEETH Sealed, Decayed Teeth stopped or extracted, and Children's Teeth regulated with care.

No. 72, Elizabeth-street, near Market-street.

Not only patients suffered pain in the early days of Australian dentistry. Youths of fifteen and sixteen, anxious to learn the trade had to make great sacrifices. Sydney Levine has two old indentures in his files. One between Arthur Cleary, dentist, and Thomas Cornwall Williams, apprentice, dated 19 October 1900, states that during the Williams' three-year apprenticeship, 'learning the art and business as dentist, he shall assiduously serve and obey the said Master night and day, and for every day he is absent without permission shall serve an extra two days at the end of his apprenticeship.'

His wages? One shilling a week for three years.

Another apprentice received six shillings a week rising to eight shillings in his final year, but his obligations to his 'Master' were considerable. According to his indentures: 'He shall not frequent taverns or alehouses, he shall not play at cards or at dice tables and matrimony he shall not contract.' It was dated 1898.

Other random facts about colonial dentistry from Levine's files: the first Australian book on the preservation of teeth was written in 1830 and amalgam was first used in fillings at about the same time. The first general anaesthetic was given to a dental patient in the 1840s when ether and chloroform were also introduced. Local, instead of general anaesthetics were first administered in the early 1900s.

Roy Underwood, an elderly retired dentist and technician was in practice during the early part of the 1900s:

'In 1906 I was eighteen years of age and I was set on learning dentistry. My father gave me a letter of introduction to Montague Alfred Noble, a dentist in Macquarie Street, Sydney and he kindly introduced me to another, named McClean. As a result I was indentured to McClean for four years to learn prosthetic dentistry. I had to pay one hundred pounds for the privilege and I didn't receive any wages.

It took me the whole four years to master the art of dental mechanics, then Mr Noble took me into his surgery to instruct me in operative dentistry.

In the first days of my surgical experience, I saw some big operations and difficult ones at that, in the removal of teeth. Often there was such a flow of blood I almost collapsed at the chairside. In those days major operations were performed by dentists in their surgeries. After a general anaesthetic, sometimes by a doctor, dentists would remove up to sixteen teeth with the patient in a reclining position in the dental chair. Often difficulties arose owing to the comparatively crude methods which were employed in those days, but after operations patients usually relaxed until such time that they were fit to go home. They received little treatment after that, and when their gums had healed they returned, impressions were taken by the dentist, and dentures made.

On a number of occasions Mr Noble was asked to operate in the home of a patient or in a Sydney hotel such as Bateman's, and I well remember seeing a barmaid collapse in that hotel from an overdose of anaesthetic. Fortunately, Noble was able to revive her but she was very close to death at one stage. Eventually, she recovered, came to the surgery, extractions were completed and we were able to make her satisfactory dentures. Her close call with death occurred in her hotel bedroom.

In those days, gold fillings were malleted into position, piece by piece, from gold foil. Sometimes it would take as long as four hours to do a big filling in a front tooth and very often, when the operation was close to completion, it would be knocked out by the dentist because of his tiredness and the work would have to be done again.

Dentures were different, too. When I began in dentistry, plates were made from gold beaten out of a sheet and it took many hours to get a reasonable degree of fit.

During my apprenticeship I was entitled to attend the Dental Hospital for practical experience. At the time it was situated above a Sydney shoe shop. I also attended lectures at Sydney University two or three times a week, while other more fortunate young men were able to spend all their time there, and when they graduated could call themselves Bachelors of Dental Surgery. They were considered to know more than people like me who had been apprenticed in the ordinary way.'

Surprisingly, the standards didn't change until as recently as 1934 when a university degree was required before anybody could practise dentistry in Australia. And at that time, according to Levine, most people expected that they would lose their teeth because of caries or gum disease by the time they were in their mid-thirties.

Bike rider and bill sticker

Bike riding and bill sticking seem an odd combination, but in the 1920s, in Sydney, it was almost a tradition among professional bike riders in slack times and for a very good reason: bill sticking was illegal, it had to be done surreptitiously in the small hours of the morning; and in a chase bill stickers on bikes had to be fast movers to keep ahead of the police who drove bikes known as 'bedsteads' and waged a constant war against them.

One of them was Joey Scruse and looking back on his life, it appears that he was always on the run. First, as a child when his father used to chase him around his backyard in suburban Leichhardt, then tie him to a tree and whip him; and when he was fourteen, on the run again, this time on a pushbike, exchanging films at great speed between Sydney picture theatres and, if time allowed, adding sound effects to silent films, tapping coconut shells on slate to imitate horses' hooves, blowing whistles and motor car horns, and by turning a handle in a six-gallon oil drum filled with broken glass giving a fair imitation of a waterfall.

I met Joey in his Paddington terrace in the late 1950s. He told me about his days 'on the run'.

'That was in 1911 and I had to ride between four suburbs exchanging the films very fast. I earned one pound a week and did it for four years. I moved over to another outfit at Annandale after that, exchanging films between only three theatres this time, always on me pushbike and always on time until one night a kid jumped from a

Joe Scruse fooling about with a bike, 1927

tram after a guard chased him off for not paying his fare. He ran right in front of me and over I went. I had two reels of film in me bag and they fell out and both rolled down the street with the film running off the spools. It took me quite a while to pick up all the film and roll it back on and by the time I got to the Strand Theatre everybody was looking for me. I was thirty minutes late.

They got the film on the projector okay and started the show but the manager got on to me. I explained what had happened and how the skin was off me arms from falling on the road. He told me to make myself scarce because the boy's father was looking for me. I took no notice, found the father instead and explained how his kid had been scaling on the tram and had knocked me over. He believed me and smacked the kid in the mouth for telling lies. I left the Strand after that and got a job at Billy Hughes' marmalade jam factory making jam for the troops serving in World War I.

About that time I joined the Western Suburbs Wheels Club. It was a time when the old penny-farthing was going out of existence. We used to train around Centennial Park on penny-farthings. They're all right, penny-farthings, but you have to sit well back in the seat to balance them . . . lean forward and you go over the front. How do you get on them? Not hard. You can hop up off a box with somebody holding the bike or by hopping up on a step fixed to the back and going as fast as you can as you sit down! Falling off them hurts!

A fashionable cyclist of the 1900s

I was a professional bike rider for twenty-five years. I built bikes too, in my shop in Oxford Street. I had a contract with Mr Nock of Nock and Kirby. His van would deliver the materials and I'd build the bikes. My four kids helped. I got £3 17s 6d each for them and Mr Nock sold them in his shop for £7 19s 6d.'

Joey Scruse raced everywhere on bikes he built, and according to his press cuttings he 'was a cyclist of great determination and a great finisher'. By 1924 he was the New South Wales track champion and the idol of the crowds.

According to his experiences on the track, how one finished in those days was almost as important as winning. He raced against the best, and before long was noticed by Bruce Small (later Sir Bruce Small) who was renowned for his famous Malvern Star bicycles.

'He hired me as a leader,' Joey said, and explained that a leader was a cyclist who got ahead of the field and then, at a predetermined point eased back to allow a prechosen winner to race through and not only give the crowds the thrills they wanted but to make sure that he was on a Malvern Star. Joe could see nothing dishonest about

A familiar scene in the 1920s

the system despite the fact that illegal betting on the races was rife. 'After all, I raced with the best,' he said. 'One of them was Hupert Opperman.'

Joey, fondly known as 'Tich' to the fans also became Australian Road Champion and Australasian Cycling Champion; his whole world revolved around bikes, and he was never far from them.

'I died in 1925. Well, that was what everybody thought, anyway. During a pile-up in a race, me and my bike ran off the track and I hit a post at the side, head first. I was unconscious for twelve days and somehow the rumour spread. Flags were flown at half-mast on the sports grounds around Sydney and my wife got lots of telegrams—they're still here in me scrapbook—and collections were taken up for wreaths, but there *was* a happy ending. She got all the money from the collections which was handy because I was dazed for a few months, wandering around; I didn't know where I was going or how I was getting there. For weeks people went white when they saw me . . . they couldn't believe it was me.

In the 1920s everybody went to work on a bike! Go out any morning and you'd see them, going to work, and then going home in the afternoon . . . going training after . . . fifty miles round Dogtrap and Parramatta . . . amateurs and professionals.

When I started training as a kid in 1913 there were hardly any motor cars and people went for long rides on bikes on Sundays, from

Sydney across Tom Ugly's punt, up to Bulli, across to Campbelltown and be back home for dinner! If anybody stopped, the rest would make a race of it and hardly stop for anything. I've seen hundreds come from Bulli down to Tom Ugly's ahead of a storm and I don't think any of them could have made it if they hadn't been in the pink of condition because it was hard. Ninety miles riding in a day with nothing but a bit of tucker in the pocket and a bottle of drink . . . but not too much!

The women used to ride, too, although they couldn't go as hard as the men. Tandems came into vogue in the early 1920s . . . boys and girls riding together.

Bill sticking was called "sniping" in 1923 when I started. I had the monopoly around Sydney and there were four other professional bike champions "sniping" for me as well: Jimmy Beer, Horace Horder, "Speed" Morgan and "Bon Bon" Franklin.

We stuck up posters everywhere . . . always in the early hours of the morning and with the coppers always after us. We had to race pretty fast sometimes to lose them, I can tell you. I dodged them for more than twenty-five years. First we'd pick up the posters from under the stage of the Tivoli Theatre where somebody printed them (a middleman got his cut) then I'd take them home and get my kids to fold them. They had to be done in a certain way so that when I started sticking I could do it fast.

The best spots around the city then were under the arches at Central and around Campbell Street. North Sydney was bad. People would take a shot at you if they caught you sticking bills around there.

Beer, Horder, Morgan and Franklin made their own arrangements, but at about two in the morning one of my kids, Joe Junior and I would go out on two bikes. We always mixed up the paste as we went. I'd take a fourpenny tin of caustic soda, and a pound of flour and we'd mix it together in a bucket of water from a public horse trough. Somehow the horse trough water was best for making paste. Then we were ready to start work on the run; me in front and Joe Junior behind carrying the posters, a brush and the paste in a cut-down kerosene tin. I'd be at it all night slapping up posters all over the place while he kept yow.* The run took us as far north as Hornsby and south down to Brighton-Le-Sands and the posters advertised just about anything you could think of.

I remember one week I got pinched seven times, and for a while we had to bail ourselves out and pay our own fines, but finally we persuaded our customers to pay half.

Fines were about thirty bob a time, but they didn't even slow us down. Sometimes I stuck up three hundred bills in a single night.'

---

* Keeping yow: watching for the police

Today, his son, Joe Scruse Junior, now sixty-eight, describes one memorable night when he was out with his father in the early 1930s.

'At that time one of the best places for posters was the side wall of the Prince Edward Theatre in Elizabeth Street. It was next to a big hole in a building site on the corner of Martin Place about thirty feet deep, and there was a narrow concrete strip about a foot wide along the length of the wall above the hole. It was enough for Dad. While I kept yow he worked his way along the wall pasting like mad and he was half-done when the coppers surprised us. Dad saw them first. "Quick! Bring the bikes!" he yelled at me.

I ran around the corner down Martin Place with them to the other end of the wall and as I did so, the coppers started working their way along the narrow strip towards Dad . . . slowly because it was a big drop into the hole. They didn't wear uniforms then . . . just big black capes over their ordinary clothes and they slowed them down a bit, but they were catching up on Dad as he got close to me waiting for him with the bikes. "Got you this time, Scrusey!" I heard them yell and they were almost on Dad when he up-ended his tin of paste on the front one and that stopped them both. He finally reached my end and we were on our bikes and away in no time.

The coppers hated Dad and me, and to tell the truth I didn't like having to do it much. Dad would never let us go out to play until we'd folded all those bloody posters. One night he did something different, but just as illegal as billsticking. The film *Zoro* was on at the pictures in town and the theatre people paid him good money to paint big Z's on the footpaths to advertise it. It was a great stunt but the police were soon on to it and they followed a trail of Z's all over town until they caught sight of Dad working in Pitt Street. They chased him round into Park Street, then down Castlereagh and caught him in Market. He couldn't deny what he had been doing; he was covered with whitewash! He got fined again.'

For better or worse, Joey Scruse senior must have led a colourful life, and Harold Stace, the famous Sydney identity in long overcoat, white gloves and dark glasses who wrote 'Eternity' in perfect copperplate with chalk on Sydney footpaths many years later seemed tame by comparison.

So do today's police compared with their more physically active kind in the 1920s who pursued the bill-stickers of Sydney on bikes. They not only made more arrests but one gets the idea that they had more fun!

My interview with Joey had been exhausting. I said goodbye and he watched as I went. I felt sorry that I left by car. If I had been riding a bike, I'm sure it would have made his day.

The silent flicks

In the rough-and-ready days of silent flicks, a film projectionist I met in the late 1950s remembered:

'I was a spool boy, but not running from theatre to theatre on a bike. I was in the biobox, where the films were shown from, at the Lyceum in Sydney. That was in 1910. In those days the film didn't run through the projector from one reel to another. It was on a single reel and my job was to wind it on to a second spool as it came off the projector. I stood to one side taking up the film and there was no question of leaving it if I got a call of nature . . . I just had to keep on winding until the reel of film was finished.

At that time a film program would consist of maybe fifteen items: scenics, a kind of newsreel, a travelogue and—surprising for that time—a nature study item showing flowers slowly opening from the time they were buds until they were in full flower. The pictures were taken then—as now—by a regular single-frame process. Another thing . . . some of the films were coloured in those days and I was told that the colouring was done by hand, one frame at a time.

I screened all of the early Australian films made by Raymond Longford with Lottie Lyle as his star. Most of them were bushranging stories with titles like *Captain Starlight*, *Captain Moonlight*, *Dan Morgan* and several others.

The price of admission in those days? Well, very low for matinees. Children could get in by bringing a couple of empty bottles. In the early 1930s at the beginning of the Depression free gifts were common at the pictures. They started by giving away small items like toasters, irons and so forth but with all the picture theatres competing with each other, things got out of hand and in the end they were actually giving away furniture . . . things costing hundreds of pounds to persuade people to go to the pictures. Then the proprietors realised it was costing them too much to compete with each other so they stopped it.

There was no censorship in those days. It was up to the exhibitor to decide what kind of film he showed, but the general standard was stricter than it is now. One film comes to mind. It was called *The Hypocrites* and in it was a woman holding a mirror up to the world and illustrating different facets of life. She was nude and seen in a kind of transparency right through the film, and before it was shown to the public I remember I screened it sixteen times to different people such as the police, ministers of religion, politicians and others in authority before they decided that most of it could be seen by theatregoers. Yet all that was cut out was about twelve frames, no more than a flash in time.

I don't know whether they all came along with censorship in mind or for a good look, ha! ha!, but if it was for the latter they were wasting their time!'

Another film projectionist started work at Murrundi, New South Wales in 1915.

'At that time the picture show was run by the local baker. My introduction into the business was delivering handbills for the shows. They didn't call them theatres in those days. Later I came to Sydney and worked for forty-two years for a motion picture trade paper and learned a lot about film-making in Australia. The first full-length feature film was made in 1899 and was called *Early Christian Martyrs.* It was produced and directed by a Mr Perry who was with the Salvation Army. Next a Victorian chemist made *The Kelly Gang* in 1906. I remember that because it was banned from showing in Victoria by the Chief Secretary's Department.

Moving on a bit I can recall some of the big film successes over the years. One of the biggest in the 1930s was a musical, *Viennese Nights* starring Vivienne Segal, Alexander Grey and Walter Pidgeon. It showed in Sydney at the Prince Edward Theatre in 1931. It was dying during the first few days and a replacement attraction had already been announced when good old reliable word-of-mouth did the trick and business picked up. It developed into a deluge and *Viennese Nights* became a record-breaker. Other big winners around that time were *Tell Me Tonight* with Jan Kiepura, and *Jack's the Boy* with the English comedian Jack Hulbert, his wife Cecily Courtnidge and Renate Muller. *One Night of Love* with the contralto Grace Moore was a big winner, too. It opened with much ballyhoo at the Liberty Theatre in Sydney.

Also in the 1930s Cinesound made a film called *The Squatter's Daughter* and Errol Flynn had a small part in it. Soon after it was finished I met him one day in Wynyard Park, Sydney and he didn't seem too happy. I asked why. "This is no place for Australian actors," he said. "I'm going to England as soon as I can."

Even then I could see that he was an actor with a future, was enthusiastic and despite an immediate lack of money had all the confidence in the world. I knew he would make good.

I remember many years ago before the talkies came in, the audience at a picture show where I was working liked a silly comedy so much they asked the manager to show it again. He did, but because he didn't have time to rewind the film, showed it on the screen upside down. The audience got down on their knees, looked back between them and laughed all over again!

Another story—and I've been assured it was true—was about a picture show in the country. It was a very cold night and there were so few people in the audience the proprietor refused to show the main feature. The patrons protested, but he was so mean he wouldn't even screen the advertising slides. He handed them around among the audience!'

Sir Edward Hallstrom, FRZS

'You can't trust black rhinos,' millionaire Sir Edward Hallstrom told me benevolently. 'But if they charge you, you must stand absolutely still and they will stop dead without harming you. That's the theory, anyhow.'

I would have found the information interesting except that we were sitting on one at the time; a two-tonne male, lying on its side in a cage at Taronga Park Zoo, Sydney, while Sir Edward scratched its ears fondly with a bunch of keys. The piggy eyes were half-closed and from somewhere deep inside came a muffled rumbling which I hoped was a sign of approval.

'It looks like a prehistoric monster and perhaps it is,' Sir Edward went on, settling back comfortably on the creature's ribs, 'the remains of some animal of thousands of years ago. Maybe a hundred thousand years ago,' he added vaguely.

I should have pressed him to be more specific, but nobody pressed Sir Edward Hallstrom for anything in 1960. He was President of Taronga Zoological Park Trust and for the past nineteen years had been its mainspring, benefactor, public relations man and boss. Taronga Park was his plaything and he had paid for the privilege with hundreds of thousands of pounds in hard cold cash.

'What Sir Edward says goes and if anybody says anything different, he goes too,' a zoo employee once told me with some feeling.

In his heyday nobody ever claimed to talk with Sir Edward; they 'humoured' him or 'handled' him and trod on eggshells when they did so.

My reason for being in the dicey situation which I have described was a Channel Seven current affairs program called 'Seven Days', and a film camera was whirring away on the other side of the wire. The item had been set up by Sir Edward who would go anywhere and do almost anything to publicise the zoo and himself; there was no perceptible difference between them, the zoo was Sir Edward and Sir Edward was the zoo. All decisions affecting its welfare were made by him.

'You see that lovely girl there—' Sir Edward pointed to a smaller vicious-looking rhino looking at us distrustingly from a far corner of the cage—'she's the female and we're hoping that the pair will mate. She's very jealous and very dangerous. Hello, she's coming this way—'

Forgetting his comforting theory about standing still, I beat a hasty retreat through the cage door with Sir Edward close behind. At the age of eighty, he looked faintly ridiculous running from a rhino, in his blue pinstripe suit, black tie, black Homburg hat and heavy horn-rimmed glasses. The door clanged shut behind us.

'I think they'll make love soon,' the old man panted. 'I know they've got their eye on each other.'

It was not the kind of comment one would expect from the chief executive of one of the world's best-known zoos, but humanising animal behaviour was a favourite trick of his, because he loved and felt close to everything that moved in Taronga Park.

For just on nineteen years he had been anathema to Australia's zoologists who regarded him as an ill-informed amateur with no academic training, whose only knowledge of animals and birds came from a lifetime of loving, observing and handling them.

For his part, Sir Edward had a pretty low opinion of zoologists and kept them out of the zoo whenever he could.

Taronga Park was one of the few public zoos which had to support itself, and time after time, Sir Edward had to come to its rescue with interest-free loans, gifts of birds and animals, even paying the staff's wages when poor gate receipts left the coffers bare. In 1943 fire destroyed the zoo's administrative block and he had a new one built at his own expense.

In return, successive state governments gave him a free hand and turned a blind eye as he slowly assumed personal control of the park and became virtual dictator over its seventy acres.

Some claimed he loved the zoo more than his family, a wife, son and three daughters. When he was acclaimed Australia's first Father of the Year in 1957, a reporter asked him for a comment on his own children.

'All the animals in Taronga Park are my children,' he said, grandly and his children were piqued, but it was partly true. Like the eagles in their tall cages, Sir Edward was monarch of all he surveyed and like them he was a prisoner, bound to the zoo by his concern for the creatures in it.

One day, at feeding time he showed me a load of fresh fruit and vegetables. 'Top quality,' he said. 'I know that some people think speck fruit and spoiled vegetables are good enough for animals, but I wouldn't allow anything here that couldn't be put on your table or mine.' The statement caused an uproar when a newspaper found out that his animals were eating better than some patients in Sydney hospitals!

His way with animals was fascinating to watch. There were few cages at Taronga Park that he could not walk into or animals he could not stroke and talk to.

He loved animals from his earliest years. Born in Coonamble, New South Wales in 1888, the son of a saddler, he kept birds in cages on the verandah of his home, even in his bedroom. When his family left Coonamble to start a new life in Sydney, Eddie was perched on top of a Cobb and Co.'s coach, clutching his most precious possessions: a tabby cat and a parrot in a cage.

Along the way the coach hit a pothole and turned over.

Nobody was hurt but the cage burst open, the parrot escaped and the cat ran off into the bush. Despite an agonising search neither was found. It was an incident he never forgot.

The family settled in Redfern where Eddie attended public school. He left when he was ten and found a job with a carpenter who apprenticed him to the trade. At the same time he was educating himself with *Harmworth Self Educators*, a set of encyclopaedias which he bought by instalments. Any spare time left was spent observing animals at Sydney Zoo, then situated at Moore Park.

He worked hard at carpentry for some years, and by 1922 had acquired a wife, a family and a furniture factory. Life was looking good, then an employee dropped dead at his work bench. It was in the days before workers' compensation, and the man's widow sued Hallstrom. She won her case and the compensation cost him his factory.

Almost destitute, he took a job selling Electrolux vacuum cleaners from door to door and acquired an ability to talk persuasively at the same time. One day a fellow-salesman told him about a new Swedish home appliance called an absorption refrigerator. Hallstrom was interested at once and soon was reading every book he could find on refrigeration. He managed to design and build a small unit of his own and struggled for months to make it work.

At three o'clock one memorable morning in 1923 he saw a rime of frost forming on the side of the unit and knew he had won. Wildly excited he woke the whole family and showed them the miracle.

Hallstrom as a young man

He built a wooden cabinet around the unit and sold it, then another and another, never buying material for a new refrigerator until he had sold the last. At the time he was so poor he once carried a refrigerator on his back for three miles, from Dee Why to Manly because he didn't have the tram fare.

As business improved he moved into a shop, and then into a disused bus depot at Willoughby where he built his first Silent Knight refrigerators, an operation which grew and grew until the factory was producing 720 refrigerators a day, or one every twenty-six seconds. And in the process, Hallstrom made a fortune.

By now he was a leading Sydney industrialist, had the ear of the state government, and when a member of the Royal Zoological Society resigned from Taronga Park Zoological Trust in 1941, it was no surprise that Edward Hallstrom was nominated for the position and got it.

A man of confidence, he soon made his presence felt among the other trustees and within a few years no decision, however small was made by anybody but him.

'Three of us practically ran Taronga Park for twenty-seven years,' Frank Purcell, aged eighty, a former trustee recalled. 'Ted, a rep. from the government and me.'

Anybody from the media who rang the zoo and asked for a statement on anything would be told 'You'll have to ring the factory and ask the "Chief".' Taronga Park was the world's only public zoo run from a refrigerator plant.

A visit there was always exciting. Hallstrom's office was situated in the middle of the place and hard to find without a guide. Crowded with stuffed birds perched on varnished branches, live birds in cages, and a featherless Mexican talking parrot which sometimes interrupted conversation, it was hard to tell where the zoo finished and the factory began.

Refrigerator parts and untidy heaps of correspondence cluttered a huge desk and behind it one found Hallstrom in the clutches of a wild animal with its mouth open, an illusion created by his unusual chair which was a large wooden carving of a brown bear, presented to him by an admirer. Overhead on a shelf was a long line of dusty boxes containing hats which had been presented to him by famous people around the world.

He suffered from persistent bronchial trouble and kept a trained nurse in constant attendance. On one occasion, I was surprised to find her attending, not Hallstrom but a baby koala which had broken its leg. Hallstrom had had the bone set by his personal physician and had immobilised the animal in a sitting position on his desk. Unable to move it had scalded its bottom and the sister was applying soothing ointment while he gently massaged its leg and talked to it softly.

He never spoke about his feelings for animals or the way he had with them, but his son John told me, 'He could tell whether a bird or animal was sick or well just by looking at it'. Two words he detested were 'millionaire' and 'philanthropist' yet he was both. Apart from his gifts to the zoo he gave away millions for medical research, and small amounts to anybody who convinced him that they needed them. He was knighted for his philanthropy in 1952.

The zoo was lucky that Sir Edward was such a superb publicist. From the 1940s till the 1960s his face was a familiar sight in Sydney newspapers and national magazines: Sir Edward holding birds, monkeys, lion cubs . . . smiling benignly in the company of the famous . . . accepting honours around the world . . . photographed in such bizarre situations as facing three fully-grown grizzly bears armed with nothing but a siphon of soda water.

One or two stunts backfired on him. One morning in an animal enclosure . . .

A typical shot of Hallstrom and an animal protégé . . . 'He was a superb publicist . . .'

'You stand there, girls and I'll stand here,' he told two attractive models in swimsuits. Towering over them was a fully-grown male red kangaroo. The cameraman focused, Sir Edward grabbed the kangaroo's paw and said, 'Now, I'll lean over like this—' Without warning, the kangaroo disengaged its paw and with a quick downward slash, clawed Sir Edward's pants right off him, leaving him bare from the waist down!

He would do almost anything to cajole paying customers into his beloved Taronga Park and greeted everybody who arrived, but not in person. There were huge photographs of him handing koala bears to Qantas hostesses on both sides of the turnstiles and just inside, in the grounds a bas-relief of his head, in bronze sculpted by his daughter, Jean Hill, together with a plaque expressing the appreciation of the trust for his years of service to the zoo. One might even see his grand-daughter, Wendy Hallstrom who was an animal keeper, or his son, John who joined the trust in 1948.

'I wasn't keen on the idea at first,' John told me when I talked with him in the 1960s. 'After all, I had spent so much of my childhood cleaning bird cages for my father, but he talked me into it.'

Sir Edward's life was like a three-ring circus with only one performer . . . himself. His drive was tremendous and he was always involved in some new project concerned with animals. With him, inspiration demanded instant action and all objections were quicky brushed aside. No wonder his critics flayed him.

He replaced the dirt floors in cages with concrete, and zoologists yelled for his blood. (Sir Edward said, 'Anybody who says dirt is more hygienic than concrete is stupid!' And that was that.) He camouflaged cages with mock sandstone—concrete slapped over chicken wire—to give them a grotto effect and was accused of turning Taronga Park into 'a concrete jungle'. He introduced Australian trout into New Guinea rivers and gave sheep to tribes in the Highlands, built up herds of pure white kangaroos by selective breeding, and sent his keepers around the world on countless trips in search of rare and interesting animals.

He imported the first gorilla into Australia, christened it King Kong and it attracted thousands to Taronga Park.

In the 1950s an elderly Sydney couple offered Sir Edward some rare paintings by John James Audubon, the famous American bird and animal painter of the nineteenth century. He bought them and decided that they should belong to the American people. He took them to the United States himself and presented them to President Harry Truman.

'Thank you,' said the President. 'Now what can I give you?'

'You can give me your hat,' Sir Edward replied. Startled, Truman did and Sir Edward brought it home and added it to his collection.

It was ironic that the man so much at home with birds and animals found it hard to communicate with his own family. His wife, a gentle woman and gifted artist who died in 1966, lived her own life and his children saw little of him.

'I think he regarded us as his possessions, and like other things he owned, put us on a shelf and left us there,' one said without rancour. He was always available for help and advice but the small pleasures he might have shared with them passed him by.

Stan Cannon, a superintendent at the zoo said, 'The watchmen used to see him wandering around the Zoo at all hours of the night, checking on the animals, making sure they were all right. One night he phoned me at home and asked me to go over and take a monkey's temperature because he thought it had pneumonia. I think he wanted another human to talk to.'

Early one morning Stan arrived at work and went straight to the giraffe house because a calf was expected. He found Sir Edward there already, bleary-eyed and ready to show him the new arrival. He had been with the mother all night and had acted as midwife.

Nobody looked forward to his visits during working hours. The 'Chief' poked into too many corners, gave too many orders and bombarded the staff with too many questions, and they did what they could to keep him out of the way. Once a junior telephonist was told to warn everybody by phone each time she saw his big black Rolls Royce, with its 'ZOO-OO' number plates roll through the tradesmen's entrance. It worked for a while, then the Chief caught on, had his chauffeur park the car outside while he sneaked into the Zoo with patrons, through the main gate.

Because he understood animals and their needs, he was a great breeder. He built up herds of black rhinos, giraffes and elan until Taronga Park possessed the largest herds in captivity anywhere in the world.

He had no luck though with macaws, the large brightly-feathered members of the bird family. Their eggs were always infertile. He gave the problem a lot of thought, decided that since the birds were by nature fast, high fliers, a lot of static electricity must have built up on their wings during flight and discharged on landing. Could this have an effect on the eggs of birds in their natural state and be absent when macaws were caged and couldn't fly at all? Typically, he didn't theorise further but built up a small battery with a low voltage output which he put in the nesting boxes. After that every egg laid by the macaws was fertile and breeding was a success.

With so much successful breeding going on, animals had to be sold or given away to other zoos. On one occasion it was decided to donate a pair of giraffes to Melbourne Zoo. One had already been caught and boxed when Sir Edward arrived and calling for a chair seated himself in the middle of the giraffe house to watch the fun while keepers chased and caught the other. It was a dangerous operation and there was only one way Sir Edward could be persuaded to leave: somebody told him he was wanted on the phone.

Next day, in Melbourne he presented the animals to the zoo trustees and heartened by the cameras and publicity which attended the ceremony, stepped forward to give the giraffes a handful of lucerne. One of them lashed out and kicked him in the face. Badly injured, he was rushed to hospital and eventually lost most of the sight in one eye, but that night, suitably bandaged he was on the plane for Sydney in time for the trustees' Christmas party at Taronga Park, where admiring guests came to pay him homage, a heady compliment which he always enjoyed.

Notably absent from such functions were most of Sydney's zoologists, whose contempt for Sir Edward had not diminished over the years. They had nothing in common with a self-taught naturalist who claimed that 'animals were their own best doctors' and 'a zoo should be a place where mothers and fathers can take their children and enjoy themselves'.

None of it was academic enough for the professionals and their day came in 1966. The New South Wales government announced that because of frequent criticism, a full-scale enquiry into the operations at Taronga Park would be held, headed by a noted Swiss zoologist and zoo director, Mr Heini Hediger.

On the day Hediger was due to arrive in Sydney, Sir Edward Hallstrom discovered that nobody had been assigned to meet him.

'He's a great man,' he told one of his daughters, 'and he should be met by somebody.' Taking her with him, he waited at the airport for three hours to greet the man who eventually would chop him down.

At the zoo, Sir Edward gave the enquiry every help he could, even inviting investigators to follow him into King Kong's cage to make a closer inspection of the animal. None of them did!

'Overcrowding' . . . 'dirty conditions' . . . 'too much concrete' . . . 'too much wire and too many bars' . . . the results of the enquiry, published in 1966 were damning and it recommended as urgent, the appointment of a professional zoologist–director to Taronga Park as soon as possible.

On the credit side, it praised Sir Edward as 'a great amateur' and said the health of the animals was good and breeding results outstanding. He reacted to the report with mixed feelings and finally threatened to take legal action but never did. Now aged eighty-one, he had observed jungle animals for too long not to know what happened when an aging leader of the herd challenged the young.

In 1967, he left Taronga Park and Mr Ronald Straughan, a senior lecturer in zoology at the University of New South Wales took his place. He got to work at once, razed the zoo's big monkey pit and dispersed its carefree inhabitants, then built a fine nocturnal house for the study of animals in its place . . . the pictures of Sir Edward disappeared from around the entrance gates, so did his bronze likeness and the plaque of appreciation; they were replaced by a duck pond.

Mr Straughan who claimed 'he didn't love animals but respected them' got rid of the children's animal circus, too, also the elephant rides and employed a number of specialists to do the work which Sir

Edward had tried to do himself. A new walk-through aviary was built and the colourful old nameplates on the cages were replaced with modern-looking ones in severe silver and black, with proper zoological information about the inhabitants.

Taronga Park Zoo had become educational at last.

Sir Edward made only one attempt to return to Taronga Park. He thought he might be of some help in the changeover and offered his services, but when he arrived at the administrative building—which he had paid for—he was rebuffed.

He retired to his small farm and private zoo at Mona Vale and for a while cared for a population of 1500 birds. At the age of eighty-three, he married again, this time to the widow of an old friend. He died eight months later. His children—then in their fifties—say he fought against it to the last, simply because he didn't want to go.

Today, those who knew him—even his children—seem privileged that they were a part—if only a small part—of his mercurial life.

Sir Edward's passion for birds and animals was almost a compulsion and puzzled many of those who came into contact with him. Perhaps only animal lovers, the kinds of people who turn away distressed when they see a stray dog facing heavy traffic on a busy street would understand.

Doris Bradshaw Blackwell

Her dressing was neat, the fashion was timeless and with her impish smile she seemed ready to step out of the photograph and say 'hello'. It's hard to believe that this delightful photograph (see page 118) of Doris Bradshaw Blackwell, aged sixteen was taken in 1907. I spoke to her in Adelaide when she was seventy-one, long after she had been witness to an exciting chapter in South Australian history. Yet the impish smile remained.

'It all started with Father's job. In 1878, when he was eighteen, he started work as a telegraphist with the GPO in Adelaide. In those days all messages and news from overseas came by cable to Port Darwin and then were sent by morse code, via repeater stations to Adelaide.

In 1899, when Father was forty, he was offered the job of officer-in-charge of the repeater telegraph station at Alice Springs. He accepted the promotion, of course and went up there to make a home for my mother, my brother Mort (five), my sister Consie (three), my brother Jack (one) and myself (eight). It was decided that we would follow him a month later.

In those days, at the turn of the century, a trip from Adelaide to Alice Springs was an ordeal, and certainly a big responsibility for Mother to have to travel a thousand miles with four small children; the first seven hundred miles by train and the last three hundred by horse and camel train over some of the roughest and loneliest country in the world. But luckily, at the age of thirty-three she was courageous and resourceful and off we went: the first one hundred and fifty miles

Doris Blackwell, aged fifteen, 1907

to Terowie by train, where we transferred to the Ghan which ran on a narrow gauge line. It was a famous train, we had a reserved carriage and apart from my family, other passengers were a Mrs Henderson and her little girl returning to her husband somewhere along the track and a governess for my brothers, sister and me.

It was a happy trip for the first part of the journey. We children were allowed to ride on the engine with the driver and if we wanted to make tea he would give us hot water whenever the train stopped. The Ghan only did about thirty miles an hour and sometimes the driver stopped to give the latest news to people who galloped up to the train on horseback. Sometimes, passengers had to tell him to 'get on with it' when he gasbagged too long.

I remember looking out of the carriage window at one stop and saw my first Aborigines. They were staring at us from the other side of the track. Many were women. I said, "Look at all the funny ladies,

The Blackwell family, just before their long trek to Alice Springs, 1899

Mummy!" Mrs Henderson corrected me at once. "They are not ladies, dear," she said, severely. "You must call them natives."

The train trip to Oodnadatta took three days and when we got there we found Father waiting with two buggies, two drivers, thirty packhorses and lots of camels to carry our belongings and us seven hundred miles to Alice Springs.

So we got going again . . . fourteen days of bouncing around on rough bush tracks and camping out each night . . . part of the journey within sight of the overland telegraph line with its repeater stations every two hundred miles between Port Darwin and Adelaide.

It seemed we were heading for the end of the world, but finally we arrived at Stuart's Creek, known today as Alice Springs.

There wasn't much there in 1899, just a hotel, two stores and three houses. All the materials required to build them had been brought three hundred miles on the backs of camels. There were only two white women at the settlement and another at a mission station eighty miles away. There were many Aborigines though watching us from the other side of the river. Their dogs welcomed us with their yelping.

Then the last short stage of our long journey, lasting for two miles along a track by the river to the telegraph station. I remember how the deep red earth sparkled with mica.

Needless to say we were glad to get there; we were bruised all over from the trip. There were only a few buildings but this would be our home for the next nine-and-a-half-years.

Apart from my family and our governess, there were four operators living on the station, also four stockmen and Alfred Lloyd, our cook. Apart from providing meals he had to make sure that our food supplies didn't run out before they were replenished by camel train in twelve months' time. Water came from a bore.

I think I should say here that some historians are wrong in assuming that the people of Stuart's Creek chose to change its name to Alice Springs. Alice Springs was simply the telegraph station then, two miles away and when the post office was transferred to Stuart's Creek, the franking stamp with "Alice Springs" on it was transferred too, and they went on using it on the mail.

Father never seemed to stop working; neither did the other operators . . . their morse keys chattered day and night as news for the newspapers came through. I remember when the first telephone conversation was held with Port Darwin, as it was called then. It was on a Sunday and I remember Father saying to me, "Now don't forget this. It is a very important occasion."

He was sworn to secrecy about what he and the other operators received and sent by code, of course, and he stuck to the rules most of the time, but sometimes, when the news was important, he would be almost bursting with it. I remember him coming into the house one morning and saying to Mother, "Well, the old lady's gone at last." He was referring to Queen Victoria who had just died. He told us all about the end of the Boer War, before almost anybody in Australia knew it, also something which was more dramatic to us—the San Francisco earthquake.

An interesting point about our home: there were holes in the walls of each room, right around it. Thankfully, neither my brothers or sister realised what they were: firing positions for rifles if we were besieged by hostile Aborigines. And all the windows were small so that none could climb in. When I was older I realised that the whole house had been designed as a small fortress.

The chance of an attack was real. Twenty-five years before we arrived a tragedy had occurred at a repeater station at Barrow Creek. The officer-in-charge, a man named Stapleton was sitting outside his station with five members of his staff and a policeman one evening, getting a breath of fresh air when a number of Aborigines crept up on them and attacked them with spears. All suffered wounds, but managed to make it back inside the buildings. Stapleton was seriously wounded. One of the operators named Flint was able to contact the Alice Springs station with details of what had happened and they were passed on to Adelaide, where a doctor gave instructions about treatment for Stapleton. He was too late; Stapleton, near death, insisted on being lifted up to a morse key from where he tapped out a final message to his wife: "God bless you and the children."

Often I felt lonely at Alice Springs because I was a good deal older than my brothers and sister, but luckily most of the people who came through visited the station because they wanted to send a telegram. Some were very unusual. One I remember was Mr de Pesco, a Romanian. He said he was a world traveller; he arrived in plus fours and was on his way from Port Darwin to Adelaide on horseback with only a black boy for company. We couldn't understand where his luggage was; we knew he must have had some because when we asked him over to the house to have tea with the family, he arrived in a dinner suit!

Of course, there was no flying doctor in those days; everybody relied on Father, and he knew very, very little about doctoring. There were frequent accidents after we got there. One man who was brought in badly injured stayed at our home for about a week while Father treated him by instruction from Adelaide. They would bring a doctor to the general post office and he would speak to the operator there who would transmit his instructions to us by morse code. Treatment was often given that way.

On one occasion Father was sent for from the township to stitch on the ear of a man who had been drinking very heavily all the week. He had tried to get up on his horse to go home and it had kicked him. Kicked his ear right off. Father just took cotton and a needle from Mother's sewing basket and went to the man and stitched the ear on again. He got nothing but abuse from the man because at the time a Doctor Chewin was at the station; he was a geologist and the man said, "Why can't he do it? He's a doctor, isn't he?" The man was very angry because Father insisted on doing the job himself.

Afterwards he told the man he mustn't touch the bandage, and he didn't because a man from the station went out much later to where the injured man lived—out in the bush somewhere—and found that he still had the dirty bandage on his head. So he took it off in horror, but found that the ear was quite all right. It had healed . . . a little crooked but was working quite well.

Mother had three children up there—two more brothers and a sister for me—and she was helped on each occasion by Mrs Myers in the township, and when she had children Mother helped her.'

Despite the drama and the hardships in Alice Springs the most memorable event each year, according to Doris was the arrival of the camel train from Adelaide, bringing everything that couldn't be carried in the fortnightly mail.

'There were thirty camels in the train and it took a lot of persuasion from their Afghan camel driver to make them kneel so that our stores could be unloaded. They carried so much . . . sugar, tea, flour, clothing, even bedding like mattresses. Everything was sorted out and put into a storeroom in lots so that it would last us for the next twelve months.

In our nine-and-a-half years at Alice Springs we had only one holiday; we went to Adelaide for nine months. We continued our schooling down there but didn't like the life at all, and afterwards were happy to return to Alice Springs with another governess for a further four years.

A very special year for us was 1907. We saw our first motor car come through. The day it arrived there was great consternation. The blacks thought it was a smoking buggy and that it was going to attack them, and the old lubras gathered their dogs together and climbed trees, and the horses in the yard stampeded and jumped the fence.

The car was a 24-horse power Talbot—we were told that—and no doubt it would look weird today. It was loaded, every inch of it, with everything needed on its journey, the first trip of its kind across the continent from Adelaide to Port Darwin. The drivers carried coconut matting—rolls of it—to help them through bogs, but as it turned out, their chief worry was hidden rocks. They were very hard on the car.

Laden down, they made two attempts to drive to Port Darwin. The first time they got as far as Barrow Creek and were in trouble. Father had given them a small telephone to connect to the telegraph wires in case they wanted help. When they told him that they were stuck he sent out a buggy, a blackfellow and horses and they came back, but the car had to stay where it was until the drivers returned a year later with another Talbot. This time one of our operators joined them and the three reached Port Darwin safely.

In 1908, I left Alice Springs and didn't return.'

Whatever happened to chemists' shops?

The old man was remembering his days as a family chemist in 1914.

'The hours I worked with Sharpe the chemist at his shop in Oxford Street were from eight in the morning until nine at night. I did it for eight years. There were only three all-night chemists in Sydney at the time.

The chief thing we sold then was castor oil. It was used for anything and everything. If you had a sore leg or a bad sprain or were constipated, castor oil was the thing . . . or glycerine . . . one or the other. And we had certain mixtures. For instance, we had a bronchitis cure that was made up in the shop. Another was a very fine ointment also manufactured by us. We tinned it and sold it over the counter. Senna tea was a favourite then, too . . . the customers bought a lot of senna in 1914.

In those days the doctor charged half a guinea for a visit. A lot of people thought it too much and came to the chemist's for treatment instead. We always obliged them, would make up something suitable and it would cost only 2s or 2s 6d. Ah, but the good old days of the chemist's shop have gone.'

They have certainly changed. Today's pharmacy is a far cry from the chemist's as many older people will remember them, with their re-assuring smells of good soap and cough mixtures, its big dispensary, the shiny ceramic jars with mysterious names like mist tussi, aconite and belladonna written on them in flowery script, the huge bottles of coloured water on display and the chemist's name and qualifications proudly inscribed on the window in gold leaf.

The dispensary in a modern pharmacy is often hard to find, hidden away like an unwanted relative somewhere at the back of the shop, and the ancient 'R' written on doctors' scripts stands not for 'recipe' any more, but for Reeboks, raincoats, rubber duckies and a hundred other items which while attracting profit would seem to be more suited to a variety store than a pharmacy.

Spanning both generations—the old and the new—was a pharmacy at Circular Quay, Sydney belonging to Douglas Ramsay which, from 1943 until 1966 represented something of both worlds. Ramsay, an outward-going kind of man, aged seventy-eight and retired, was both chemist and 'doctor' to a quarter of a million locals and ferry commuters who sometimes queued up for his advice and treatment.

Among his extra-curricular activities on Monday mornings—the busiest time—syringing of ears, dressing cut feet, bathing sore eyes and giving adrenalin shots to asthmatics. There was no objection from local doctors, he says. Some even sent patients around to him sometimes when they were busy.

'The 1930s, 1940s and 1950s were the great days of patent medicines and the advertising hype that accompanied them. Pills and bottled medicines were available for just about every human complaint, and for some which nobody had thought of; unlike today, manufacturers could make extravagant claims for any product without fear of prosecution.'

But none of Ramsay's experiences as a chemist at Circular Quay equalled his performance in the 1930s when, as a young man, he was largely responsible for the creation of a patent medicine which took Australia by storm.

At the time, Beechams Pills were worth 'a guinea a box', a number of tonics claimed to prevent a dread condition they called 'mineral starvation' and a slogan for Laxettes proclaimed that users were 'happy and gay, the Laxette way' although it was doubtful whether anybody would be happy about having to buy laxatives in order to stay regular. Bonningtons, which advertised its Irish Moss cough mixture for years proudly claimed that the secret of its success was 'Pectoral Oxymel of Carrageen' an extract from seaweed 'found off the north coast of Ireland'. Apparently the Irish hadn't heard of its beneficial properties because they were believed to suffer from as many colds as anybody else, and the same with Buckleys Canadiol Mixture which was heavily advertised on Australian radio. The commercials began with a windy blast and the words, 'Up in the wilds of blizzardly cold Canada—' and went on to claim that 'coughs and colds didn't stand Buckleys with Buckleys Canadiol Mixture,' although it was likely Canadians had never heard of the stuff.

Then a brand-new product hit the market. It was called 'Bidomak: the Tonic in a Bottle'. In terms of sudden acceptance by the Australian public and the massive profits it produced, nothing equalled Bidomak in the 1930s, a reminder that not a lot had changed since persuasive medicine men sold coloured water from their horse-drawn wagons to gullible yokels in the early days, or until today, when advertising agents practise much the same hokum in pushing medicinal products.

The Bidomak saga began with Sydney Oscar Beilby, an aggressively competitive Adelaide grocer who, by dint of hard work had built up a chain of forty grocery stores in city and country.

Always on the move, he got fed up one day with packing and selling other firms' pharmaceutical products and decided that there would be more profit in manufacturing and distributing them himself. He knew nothing about the business and advertised for a manufacturing chemist to get the project started.

Douglas Ramsay, then in his twenties had just completed a four-year course in pharmacy at Adelaide University with commerce afterwards. He saw the advertisement, applied for the job and was called in for an interview.

Ramsay says his first impression of Beilby was 'of a middle-aged, uninteresting and poorly-educated man who wore spectacles with very thick lenses'.

However, there was nothing thick about Beilby. As Ramsay would find, he had the gift of being of being able to pick the right man for the right job and to make decisions quickly. It was an important part of his success and within a few minutes Ramsay was hired at a salary of £10 per week.

Neither man could have foreseen the dramatic result of their meeting and how it would make Beilby a multimillionaire within just a few years. Ramsay recalls:

'My first job was to set up a production plant and testing laboratory, then with the help of an elderly industrial chemist I set about manufacturing iodine tincture, friar's balsam, fluid magnesia and other nostrums. In 1935 we decided to try making a patent medicine.

Clement's Tonic had held the top position among tonics in Australia for years, and a challenge to it seemed a likely way to go. Parrish's Chemical Food was another popular over-the-counter product so the other chemist and I devised a formula somewhat similar to the latter, but about three-quarters of its strength. We added some other components and flavoured the result with coccus cacti, an extract from a dried beetle which gave it a good red colouring.

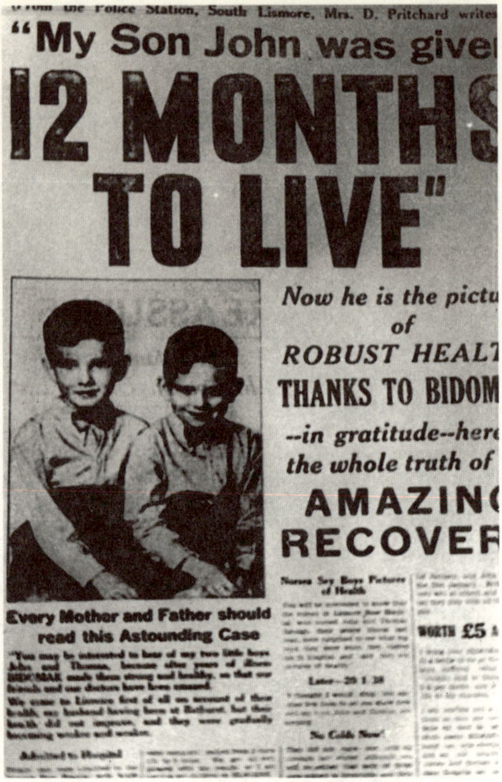

Instant longevity at 3s 6d a bottle

We called it Bidomak: the Tonic in a Bottle. I don't remember where the name came from but Bidomak sounded catchy. Production started and our employer, S.O. Beilby was so impressed he issued an order to each of his forty shop managers that they had to sell a dozen bottles a week or be sacked. It was typical Beilby. Fear won out and some managers sold a dozen or more above their quotas and were suitably rewarded by Beilby who appreciated initiative. It was labelled "The Tonic of the Century"—nobody, as far as I know ever questioned that extravagant claim—and it sold for three shillings a bottle in South Australia. Demand for Bidomak grew at a promising rate and shrewd S.O.B. allotted ten pence from every sale for advertising.

As a result, the acceleration of sales in South Australia and Victoria was amazing, but in New South Wales it was a boomer! At three-and-six a bottle, New South Welshmen couldn't get enough of the stuff. New Zealand was another lucrative market. Premises were rented in Wellington and I went over to get the show on the road. The nett profit from the first year's sales in New Zealand was £127 000.

When I presented the figure to Beilby and he saw that lots of equipment used in the production of the "tonic" and no longer required had been sold at a profit, he told me that I had been mean, then smiled and presented me with a bonus of £1000.

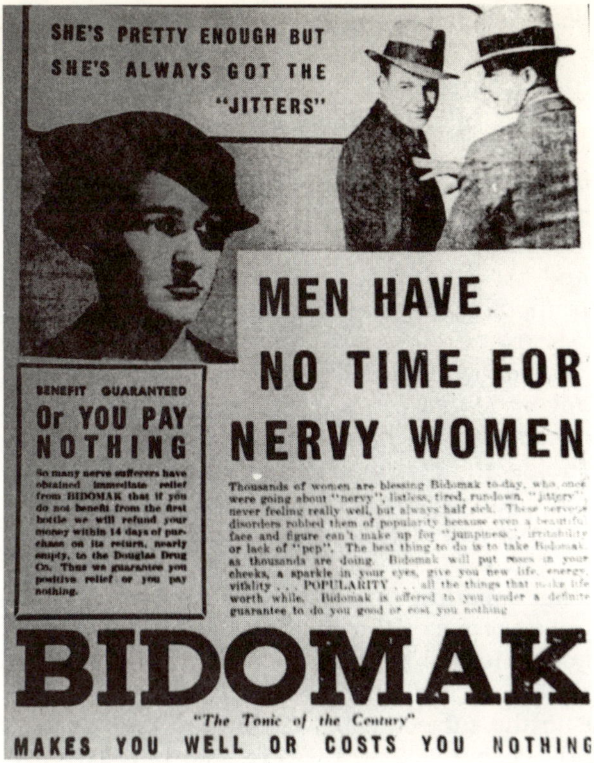

The key to romance? Bidomak!

Sales kept on increasing. All of Australia seemed to feel the need for a tonic and Bidomak filled the bill. Hundreds of testimonials came in from grateful customers, claiming all kinds of wonderful results, from the elimination of warts to frequent erections, according to one satisfied customer who said it had saved his marriage.

By 1936, I saw the need for a factory in Sydney and told Beilby so at an action meeting one Friday afternoon in Adelaide. He said, "You've made your point. Fix it!" So I went to Sydney and within a few days had bought land in Pelican Street, drawn a sketch plan of the kind of factory we needed on a bit of graph paper for an architect and the project started. Within a comparatively short time we were manufacturing Bibomak in New South Wales. Fifty girls were engaged to pack the product, and advertising it became big business with double spreads in the *Sydney Morning Herald*, health talks on radio stations and so on.

By now Beilby was on cloud nine and rich beyond his dreams. He moved to Sydney, bought a three-storey residence on three hundred feet of water frontage around the corner from the prime minister's Sydney residence at Kirribilli. It had tennis courts, a lift and a large ballroom. He took up dancing, socialised heavily and my wife and I were made a part of it. We lived a short distance away at Neutral Bay and it was not uncommon for Beilby to phone me any night around six o'clock and say, "We are dancing tonight. How is your wife's hair? Black tie . . . the car will pick you up at eight!" There was tennis too at his home, or commands to play bridge with small groups of business people. There was always dancing afterwards, with a five-piece band and a uniformed butler in attendance to serve champagne. He liked dancing but was peg-legged and no good at it.

It was a far cry from his life in Adelaide as a humble grocer to the razzle dazzle of Sydney and his rather high social profile as owner of the most successful patent medicine in Australia, so it was no surprise when he sold his grocer shops.

Too much to enjoy in Sydney to bother about groceries. And of course, there were his dancing lessons . . .

It was the dancing and Beilby's own drinking that did it. Early in 1939, leaving his wife at home and accompanied by his lady dancing teacher, he set sail for South America but by the time they reached New Zealand, war with Germany seemed so certain that he decided to return to Australia.

For some time prior to his departure I had been reminding him of the need to stockpile supplies of material to make Bidomak. I tackled him again when he got back. He had taken to hitting the scotch bottle when under pressure and he was in a filthy mood when I faced him in his office and brought up the subject again. He abused me for making such demands and became violent. I hadn't seen him like that before and I didn't like it so I quit . . . walked out and didn't see him again. But it had been an extremely interesting four years.'

Some months later, at the age of fifty-five and well primed with Johnny Walker, Beilby fell down a stairway in his home, suffered a heart attack and died. One way and another, the ship, now without Ramsay or its owner, faltered, got off course and foundered. 'The tonic of the century' had had its day.

'History is full of the meteoric rises and falls of potentates and politicians,' Ramsay muses, 'but a patent medicine? Very rare.'

I had a last question for Ramsay—I asked him about the efficacy of Bidomak, its real value as a tonic.

He gave me a hard look. 'Don't make me laugh,' he said.

The bushrangers: terror on horseback

They ravaged the Australian countryside for almost one hundred years. They stole, pillaged and murdered, staking their liberty and lives on the speed of their horses (usually stolen) and the threat of their guns. Always on the run, they led a will-o'-the-wisp existence in and out of the bush, often with squads of police and armed settlers close behind.

No farmer was safe from them, no coach with passengers and mail could be guaranteed a safe passage from one part of the country to another without a sudden cry of 'Bail up!' or 'Halt! I have a gun on you!' from bushrangers; and a consequent loss of mail, valuables and even life. Poor communications, scattered settlements and the cartage of large sums of money and gold by road were all the incentive they needed.

Two telegrams sent from New South Wales country post offices to headquarters in Sydney in the 1860s and which were shown to me at the Post Office Museum were typical of many. One, dated 6 November 1862 reads:

> TO THE POSTMASTER GENERAL. MAIL FROM BATHURST TO HARTLEY ROBBED LAST NIGHT NEAR WOODSIDE. COACH STOPPED TWICE BY THREE ARMED MEN. ALL MAILBAGS OPENED AND RIFLED.

Another, dated 6 August 1867:

I BEG TO REPORT THAT THE MAIL TODAY FROM MERRIWA WAS STUCK UP BY THUNDERBOLT AND HIS BOYS ABOUT FOURTEEN MILES BEYOND DENHAM. ALL BAGS RIFLED.

Most of the bushrangers were 'bolters', convicts who had escaped from road gangs and settled for a freer but chancier existence in the bush; all were desperate men; the threat of a trooper's bullet or capture and death at the end of a rope hung over each twenty-four hours of every day.

Jimmy Governor was different from most. He was part-Aborigine, had been born in Australia and although his bloody career as a bushranger in the late 1890s lasted only three months he quickly gained a reputation as the most brutal of all. His lawless activities covered an area of more than a thousand square miles from Albury to Gulgong, and included nine murders, six rapes and more than one hundred lesser crimes.

Before his life of crime Governor worked as a farmhand for a settler named Mawby and at that time met and married a white woman named Ethel. Mawby's wife objected and made her thoughts known in public. One evening, Governor, bent on revenge and accompanied by a mate, Jackie Underwood, burst into the Mawbys' farmhouse and wielding a tomahawk killed not only Mawby and his wife but three other women and a small boy as well.

No turning back after that. Encouraged by his wife Ethel, who saw bushranging (and easy riches) as his only option, Governor, with his brother Joe and Underwood took to the bush.

When the murders were discovered at Mawby's place, scores of regular police together with special constables who had been sworn in began a determined hunt for the trio, but instead of lying low Governor and his companions continued on a bloody rampage across the country. Seeking food they approached an isolated farmhouse. A young woman carrying her baby son came out and asked, 'What do you want?'

'You should be more civil, missus,' was all Governor said and shot both dead. The three stole supplies and left but not long afterwards they were sighted by police, and a skirmish ensued. Jackie Underwood was disabled with a single shot (he was later tried and hanged) but Governor and his brother Joe managed to escape.

Their next confrontation was with an old man on a farm near Gulgong. They bailed him up, stole his horses and rifle, and although he offered no resistance, Governor shot him dead before the pair rode off.

By now a reward of £2000 was offered for their capture, dead or alive, yet there was still no stopping them. Rapes and more murders by Governor were reported and soon two hundred mounted police

Police officers in bushranging days led a dangerous and lonely life

had joined the hunt, while two thousand armed volunteers guarded isolated homesteads.

The fugitives, who were finding it increasingly hard to steal food and fresh horses came upon a hut on the Forbes River. It looked deserted, but unknown to them it was occupied by police. In the sudden exchange of fire which followed, a constable was wounded and Governor and his brother ran for their lives.

The police were close behind however, and in another exchange Jimmy was shot in the hip. Another shot tore out four of his teeth. Yet both men escaped again and soon after decided to separate. (There is no record of what eventually happened to Joe.)

Twelve days later a stroke of luck for the police. A constable sighted Governor camped in the bush not far from a farm owned by a man named Wallace. Instead of confronting him, he returned to the homestead, organised men and guns, and with Wallace and seven local farmers returned in the early hours of the morning to where the bushranger lay asleep near the remains of his campfire. They surrounded him.

At dawn, Governor woke and stood up, then ignoring previous instructions from the constable and Wallace, a farmer named Green showed himself and called on Governor to surrender. Governor tried to run, but Green shot him, so did the others and Governor fell to the ground, unconscious.

Later, a police surgeon found that he had been hit more than twenty times, yet he lived.

He appeared under heavy guard in court at Wingham later, was remanded to Sydney, tried, found guilty of his crimes and hanged at Darlinghurst Jail on 18 January 1900. He was twenty-six.

Fifty years later I met and talked with Richard Hammond, then an historian and research officer with the New South Wales police force. He said that Governor's savage record as a bushranger had modified a commonly-held opinion at the time, that bushrangers were entitled to a measure of sympathy. In the minds of some they were regarded as romantic figures.

Even Governor Macquarie, in a statement he made in 1823 said, 'I have no doubt that many convicts who have, or might have been rendered good and useful had they been treated with reasonable control, have taken themselves to the woods where they can only subsist by plunder, and many of whom have had their lives terminated on the gallows.'

Little wonder that bushrangers were assured of food and a night's lodging by simple folk who saw them, not as criminals but underdogs like themselves, victims of the undoubtedly hard times and deserving of consideration.

Hammond said, 'There was rough justice in the view. After all, many had led respectable lives in England and Ireland until some trivial crime had brought them down, resulting in transportation to Australia, where cruelty by their jailers had demeaned and hardened them.'

Reports of holdups in the 1860s support Hammond's opinion that not all bushrangers were merciless villains bent on terrorising innocent travellers.

One reads 'The three bushrangers were recognized as members of Ben Hall's gang. They were Messrs Gilbert, O'Meal and Johnny Vane. All were fashionably dressed and looked and acted like gentlemen.'

Others tell of 'bushrangers allaying women travellers' fears,' of questioning poorer passengers and taking only part of their valuables or money, and thanking passengers profusely for their 'co-operation' before riding off.

A report of how bushrangers held up the Goulburn Mail:

> At three o'clock on Thursday afternoon the mail was stopped about a mile on the Sydney side of Badgerry's Inn at Bargo Brush by two armed bushrangers, well-mounted with two double-barrelled fowling pieces and two pocket pistols. They deliberately rode up and addressing themselves to the coachman said, 'Stop the mail!'

The Cooma to Bombala Mail Coach, 1907

> One immediately alighted, requested that the mail bags be thrown out, which they commenced without loss of time to open by cutting the fastenings; one or two seals were broken but they didn't find any money, and returned the letters.
>
> They were very civil to the passengers, took £7 from Mr Frederick Jones, £2 of which they returned, to bear his expenses on the remainder of his journey to his station.
>
> They detained the Mail about ten minutes then wished the travellers 'Good day' and rode off towards Sydney. Upon the whole, and under all circumstances, they were very decent highwaymen. Before they left they also opened a pair of saddlebags and took away a Jim Crow hat which gave them a hearty laugh.

However, the sneaking or open regard which travellers felt for bushrangers was not shared by all, some of whom felt that normally-decent young men growing up in the colony might follow their unlawful example and take to the road. In a furious letter to the authorities an irate settler claimed 'There is scarcely a house between Mount Macquarie and the Abercrombie River that will not afford any criminal shelter when required. I am convinced that there are hundreds of lads under twenty who would give their eyes to have the same notoriety as Gilbert and Gardiner, two of Hall's gang. They never work, never have worked and without doubt are the flashiest I ever did see!'

There was an alarming peak in bushranger activity from 1829 to 1831 when no less than five hundred 'runaways' and 'bolters' escaped from iron gangs, armed themselves and sought easy pickings. Not all were successful. During the period, one hundred and fifty were caught and executed, fifty-two of them in 1829 and the others the following year. Among the most notorious: one Jack Donohue, long sought by the police and shot dead in 1830 by a constable who caught him in a patch of scrub outside Campbelltown.

Yet the situation remained critical. Governor Darling, in a statement he made at the time expressed his concern about the deterioration in law and order, and the dangers involved in pursuing and apprehending offenders. Couched in even the restrained officialese of the day, his report loses none of its drama:

> A gang of from twelve to fifteen, assembled at Hunter's River plundered the settlers of horses, arms, etc., and with difficulty was driven from that part of the country, it having been impossible to come up with them after the first skirmish, in which three of them were killed.
>
> Also, I am sorry to say, another thirteen in the Bathurst district have recently risen and plundered neighbouring farms of necessary equipment. Well armed and provided with stolen horses they were pursued by parties of troops and mounted police but I regret to say the latter were beaten off with a loss of two men and five horses after a smart quarter of an hour's engagement.
>
> Such incidents depress the settlers and many, in the first moments of alarm quit their farms. I lost no time in sending reinforcements of troops to furnish guards over the convict gangs and road parties, as should these people rise, who are fifteen hundred in number, the consequences might prove of the most serious nature.

Despite the best efforts of the administration to keep the situation under control, bushranging activity increased and rose to new heights between 1862 and 1870 when twenty people, either civilians or police were murdered, and by 1879 thirty-five troopers had either been killed or seriously wounded.

Between 1878 and 1880 the infamous Ned Kelly and his gang, whose crimes included robbing two banks and holding up two townships, added to the carnage by killing six people. Their lawless reign ended when they made and donned crude armour and shot it out with police at a small hotel in Glenrowan. Kelly was taken and later hanged.

Not surprising, in the light of the dangers involved, that recruits for the police force were hard to find. Many who joined had to work alone, they were spread thinly across the country and got little support from the people they were supposed to serve. Also, their superiors expected them to use fear and intimidation in the maintenance of law and order, to be judge and jury when a crime was committed and the offender caught. They were expected to administer floggings, also.

Hammond said:

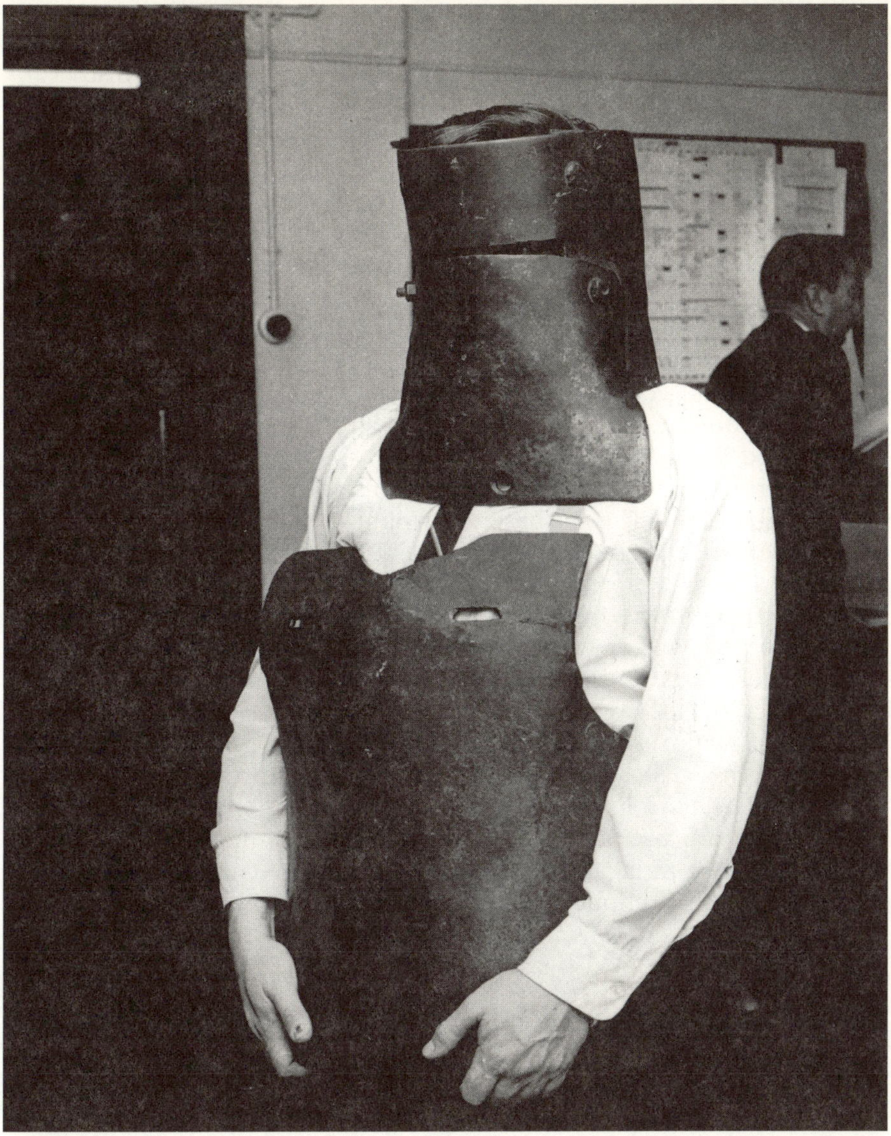

Headpiece and breast-plate from one of the armour suits made by the Kelly gang from quarter-inch ploughshare steel, modelled here by a police officer

'Free settlers made better money in trade, and often the only recruits available were convicts, resulting in a situation where bushrangers, nearly all of whom were former convicts were pursued by other convicts now in uniform, often men who had come out on the same ship with them.

Again, police had to travel great distances on horseback to deliver subpoenas or on other business, and while they were away bushrangers could descend on a town, commit outrages and be gone by the time the constable got back. In fact, in the mid-1860s they didn't much care whether the constable was there or not; for instance, one gang rode into town, went straight to the police station, shot the constable dead then rode away.

Later, the Clarke brothers who terrorised the Nerrigundah district were responsible for the massacre of four special constables who had been sent out to deal with them. Many bushrangers appeared to lead a charmed life, like the infamous Captain Thunderbolt—real name Frederick Ward—who terrorised the New England district around Uralla, had a hideout in the mountains and was on the loose for ten years.

However, his career came to an end one day after he had held up an inn outside Uralla. One of the locals who was drinking there was able to sneak away, ride into town and raise the alarm. A number of constables, led by one named Walker galloped out to the inn at once. Thunderbolt had gone but they were able to follow his tracks over some very rough country and finally caught up and cornered him at a place called Kentucky Ponds.

Thunderbolt was on one bank and Constable Walker and party were on the other. The bushranger, well armed and ready to fight yelled, "Don't throw it all away on me. Think of your wife and children!" Walker ignored him, charged straight into the water and shot the other's horse from under him. Even then Thunderbolt refused to give up and Walker was forced to shoot him dead.

Then there was Ben Hall. He was almost a legend. Some believed that he was a settler who had been forced into bushranging after his wife ran off with a policeman, and other police were always baiting him, letting his cattle out of the yards on his property and so on, so he took to the road in revenge. A nice story, but in retrospect it's clear that he was as much a hardened criminal as most of the others.

He was a real thorn in the side of police. They chased him for three years. The continued operation involved the deployment of many men, much money and when they got him finally, his end was brutal. A Sergeant Davidson and party, led by a black tracker found him asleep in a patch of scrub outside Forbes and they pumped no less than sixteen bullets into him. Later, they claimed that he had gone for his guns.

Few settlers believed their story, and there was even less support for the police after that. Before long, Hall had become the hero and police the villains in the minds of many settlers. Indeed, a ballad about it was written, circulated and became popular. It went:

> Come all Australian sons with me
> For a hero has been slain
> Cowardly butchered in his sleep
> Upon the Lachlan Plain.
> Yes they savagely murdered him
> The cowardly bluecoat imps
> Who only found his hiding place
> From sneaking Peeler's pimps.

There's a depressing footnote to Hall's death. After the killing, his body was put on public view at the local lockup and girls who had admired him in life, snipped locks from his beard as they filed past . . .'

Such gruesome details deserved a moment's silence, even fifty or sixty years after. I looked around me. We were standing among dusty heaps of old papers, reward notices, dog-eared books and faded photographs. On a shelf nearby were the deathmasks of two bushrangers. Surprisingly, neither wore the agonised expressions one would expect to see on the faces of men who had just spent their last moments on the scaffold. Both were tranquil; indeed one wore the faintest suspicion of a smile as though he had seen something not visible to the living left behind.

Another moment and I might have started thinking about man's inhumanity to man but Hammond had moved on, and was talking now about how Australian bushrangers operated.

'Early on each tended to work alone, but later they acquired accomplices and some, like Ben Hall, formed gangs of five or six and there were even larger groups. One at Ugarra Rocks staged a holdup with ten men.

Very few lived to old age. Most of them were prepared to accept bushranging as a life, knowing that at the end there would be an inevitable confrontation with police. Most were shot dead or hanged while still in their early twenties.'

As he talked, they seemed to merge into one . . . the good and the bad, the guilty and the innocent . . . the senseless murders on one side matched by the 'just' killings on the other. From the moment a judge a world away brought down his gavel until a hangman released the trap in far off Australia, the course was set for many, while for others it was a life in chains with the lash at the ready for the slightest insubordination.

Bushrangers, settlers, police and convicts alike were the victims of the harsh period in which they lived. It had brutalised them all.

Before I said goodbye to Hammond, he showed me a rope which had been used to hang many bushrangers in New South Wales. It was of rough twisted hemp, but surprisingly, the noose itself was encased in a soft leather sleeve.

Not much compensation for a man about to die at the end of it, but it did provide a welcome hint of compassion.

The entertainers

The houselights dim, the audience quietens, a quiver of excitement runs through the theatre, then that exquisite moment of anticipation just before the curtain rises on another live performance.

Or that was how it was before the flicks and later, television, moved in. The matinee idols, the grande dames, the heroic actors and knockabout comedians who graced the Australian stage sixty, seventy and eighty years ago have long gone; but forty years ago, some of them, retired and with only the memory of past triumphs and the applause of the crowd for company, were still around.

One of them was diminutive Mrs Coutts. She thought she was in her late seventies, but wasn't sure because her birth had never been recorded. She agreed to talk about her experiences in Australian show business when she was a child. With some pride, she told me:

'My mother and father were both theatricals. Mother was a dancer and danced with Mrs J.C. Williamson (her maiden name was Weir) and my father accompanied her. My first stage appearance was at the Princess Theatre in Melbourne in the early 1880s when I was four years of age. My stage name was Phyllis Ferrier and I did a speciality act. I wore a long flowing frock and I sang "Daddy". After the performance the permanent first-nighters sent me down their floral tribute.

When I was five my mother and father parted company and my father brought me to Sydney and he started a tour of outback country towns. We travelled everywhere together in Cobb and Co. coaches. We showed in some of the towns on the goldfields; many of them were just tents. We played in a big tent usually and sometimes in hotel dining rooms. We carried the show on our backs, my father and I.

We did all kinds of things to entertain: we played musical instruments, including the bottles and bells and a xylophone, we did sketches together and he did a sleight of hand act in which I assisted him. I did song and dance and recitations, also. When Father was on the stage alone I would be outside somewhere changing my costume.

I did all kinds of things like that with my father from the time I was five until I was thirteen.

Whenever we did a second night in a town we did thought-reading which I hated. I was so tensed up. I had to gaze into a little piece of metal which my father gave me and with which he sent me into a trance. (I was not in a trance.) Then he blindfolded me and going out into the audience would select something and say "What am I holding?"

I would have to say, "A watch". What was difficult though was getting the numbers on a watch.

In a way it was trickery, but finally I found myself beginning to get a passage of thought from Father. He didn't know it, because I never told him, but before he would say anything I would know what he was holding but would have to wait for his question before giving the answer.

You may wonder how I got my education during those years. Well, my father was a well-educated man and he was my schoolmaster. We lived in hotels and so that I could study quietly he used to lock me in my room.

I remember one of the tent towns we visited as if it were yesterday. The only building in it was the hotel where we stayed, and when we gave our performance we had to use a dining-room table for a stage and tablecloths for curtains.

But the miners were nice . . . they were very kind to me and I used to thoroughly enjoy myself.'

A dancer

One of the ironies of living in Kings Cross, Sydney is that in spite of its frenetic atmosphere and reputation as a centre of excitement for the young, it can be a lonely place for the elderly, many of whom knew it at a time when it was the haunt of actors, artists and writers, generations before teenage runaways, drugs and a variety of crimes required police patrols on its streets day and night.

Miss Leach was one of them. Although somewhat frail, she radiated dignity and independence, and had spent most of her working life in the theatre.

'I am an elderly person, quite elderly, being over eighty and probably with one foot in the furnace, but I'm not going to be thumbed down yet awhile.

I was a ballet dancer with J.C.Williamson from 1908 until 1919. Most of the time I was in pantomime which was big then. Pantos were very lavishly mounted with wonderful casts: the famous actress Florence Young was our principal boy most of the time and Fanny Dango was principal girl.

In those days pantos seemed to be more popular with adults than with children. Shows were booked out night after night; they had big casts and imported costumes. There were fifty girls in the ballet and about the same number of chorus girls and a smaller number of showgirls.

There was no classical ballet in Australia at that time, but the ballet schools were excellent: Jenny Brennan's in Melbourne and Minnie Hooper's in Sydney. Looking back I realise that they were both very good teachers. Very few male dancers in my day, only eccentric dancers like Clyde Cook and Eddie McLean . . . girls took the male parts . . . men considered it sissy to be ballet dancers.

I was in one or two shows with Bland Holt. He was a famous producer in his day and his shows were tremendously popular. Everything that could be done for realism on stage was done. If he wanted cows in a production they were there with girls from the country to milk them . . . horses too. Each time they were included we danced in horse manure a lot of the time.

I remember I was in one of Mr Holt's shows called *The Bondsman* and George Rignold, a famous leading man of the past was in it. He was "getting on" as they say, and in the final scene he had to read a letter. He always made the most of it and we never knew how long he would take . . . we all wanted to get off the stage and go home.

In that show we had a harvest ballet with horses. To us it seemed that they deliberately held back until the performance, then they let go. It made dancing difficult.'

Violet Elliott, actress

The tattered old theatre program dated 25 January 1909, announced that the Cremorne Theatre was proud to present the Harry Rickard Vaudeville Company, and among some notable artists mentioned on the bill was 'Miss Violet Elliott (the miniature Marie Lloyd) $7\frac{1}{2}$ years old.'

I met Violet in 1968. She had been trained in childhood to speak and sing to audiences in big theatres and her voice was as rounded and beautiful as it must have been during her varied career as a fat-girl comic, an acrobat, a dancer and a principal in musical comedy. Digging into her family history Violet said:

'I go back to the time when theatre charges were sixpence for a seat in the gods and ten shillings for a box. I first went on stage at the age of two and a half at a theatre in Western Australia. On the same bill were my father, Arthur Elliott and my mother Maude Fanning. She was a well-known impersonator.

Ours was a dyed-in-the-wool theatrical family, parents and children travelling together. Every year Mama seemed to have another child and we were put on the stage and went to school wherever my parents played. I think I attended more convent schools than any other child. Mama had seven children altogether while the family was travelling—two died—and the five of us went on the stage. One of my sisters, Lulla Fanning became very well-known.

I stayed with Mama's act until I was sixteen, then I branched out and worked in revues, travelling pantos and vaudeville. I made one or two early Australian films then joined Stanley McKay for four years with a travelling panto. We showed all over the place. On Saturday afternoons we had to play Shakespeare for Mr McKay.

Those were the days when Australian theatrical artists got a real grounding and whatever talent they had in them was brought out, encouraged, and anybody who wasn't good wasn't heard of again.

I had to be able to sing and dance, play parts in drama and do sketches in revues. My mama taught me voice production because she had already been taught herself. In those days there were no microphones; if you couldn't be heard clearly up in the gods you were out of work. Before I went to England in 1930 I played with the biggest artists in Australia: Roy Rene, Fred Bluett, Madge Elliott and Cyril Richard, Jim Gerald and George Wallace.

Theatrical folk have always been superstitious . . . so many taboos, like whistling in the dressing room, for instance. If you do you have to go outside, knock on the door three times and ask if you can come back in. On one occasion I was playing farce in a theatre which was said to be haunted by the ghost of a woman who had once owned it.

Well, one night I had finished the show, the curtain came down and everybody went home, but for some reason I was late getting cleaned off and I was about to leave the theatre via the auditorium. Going up the aisle towards the front door, I stopped and looked back towards the stage as I often did and I thought to myself how dark and drab and dreary the place looked without an audience and I thought of all the laughter that had been heard there during the evening's performance. The theatre seemed to take on a different kind of spirit—it was lifeless like a body without a soul.

I was about to turn away when I saw something. I had another look to make sure and I tell you that what I saw was a ghost. It was a woman's figure—grey—dressed in what looked like a very old theatrical costume with chiffon sleeves hanging down. Her hair looked like green seaweed. She was sitting in a box on prompt side, looking down at the empty stage as if she was engrossed in a bygone play.

Believe me, I couldn't get out of the theatre quickly enough . . . it took me about five seconds!'

Irene Nelson, ballet girl

Violet Elliott's early experience with Stanley McKay's travelling tent show was usual then for ambitious young Australians who wanted to make a life for themselves in the theatre. His revues under canvas were big business and brought entertainment to country towns and cities up and down the east coast of Australia from the turn of the century until the early 1940s.

George Sorlie was another prominent entrepreneur with a travelling show and both, presented in huge tents, lacked none of the variety or sophistication of those in theatres in the city.

Irene Nelson, aged sixty-nine, took her first dancing lessons with Francis Scully's School of Dancing when she was three, and joined McKay's company as a ballet dancer in 1937 when she was fifteen.

'It was an exciting life for a teenager, and the shows were marvellous. There were ten girls in the ballet, an orchestra of six and topline comedians and variety acts. When the show hit a country town and the big tent went up everybody came; it was packed every night.

After a while with McKay's I was offered a chance to audition for George Sorlie's show. It was successful and because it suited me better I changed over. Both Mr Sorlie and Mr McKay were good businessmen and kept an eye on the pennies. Ballet girls were provided with costumes of course, but we had to buy our own makeup. And most people in the company had to double-up. Sometimes we had speaking parts in dramas like *East Lynne*, and even the tent boys who helped to erect the big tents sold lollies to the audience during intervals. I remember Mr Sorlie owned a big supercharged Auburn car and when he drove into a country town everybody knew his show couldn't be far behind.

Naturally, boys in country towns were always trying to get off with us ballet girls, but Aunty Grace (Mrs Sorlie) was very strict; she insisted on meeting every boy who wanted to take us out anywhere, and if a girl disgraced herself or got mixed up in any hanky panky Aunty Grace had her put on the first train back to Sydney and she wasn't seen again!

It didn't stop me, though. In 1940, when I had been dancing with Sorlie's for three years, I met a boy in uniform in a Newcastle cafe.

He was stationed at Greta camp. I was seventeen, he was nineteen, we fell in love and got married. I left the show and we stayed happily married until he passed on 48 years later.'

Stanley McKay, travelling showman

Stanley McKay was Australia's most famous travelling showman. Born in Tumut, New South Wales in 1877, McKay's first job was in a bank, but he had only one real interest: the theatre. At the age of twenty-two, when he could stand the monotony no longer, he quit and formed a small theatrical company.

On its opening night in Mudgee enough customers turned up to produce a profit, which was lucky because by the time all the expenses had been paid, the young entrepreneur had only two shillings left!

There was no going back after such a heady start; it marked the beginning of a long and often adventurous career in show business. For the next sixty-three years McKay's mobile theatre brought a range of wholly-professional entertainment to country folk and his big tent was a familiar sight in country towns all the way from northern Queensland to Tasmania.

When World War I broke out in 1914, McKay first fulfilled all his contracts then folded his tent for the duration, and with every male member of his company returned to Sydney where they joined the forces together.

From reports, his war service, active enough, was mild compared with some of the difficulties he encountered when he returned after the armistice and took up where he had left off five years before, touring the eastern coast of Australia and New Zealand with dramas, musicals and the rest.

According to Arthur Sullivan, writing in *The Outdoor Showman*, McKay and his company were shipwrecked in New Zealand and escaped with nothing but the clothes they stood up in and the loose change in their pockets. Bushfires, hurricanes and other natural disasters added to the occupational hazards of taking a show out on the roads of Australia. Like the time a punt carrying his motor lorries and all of his theatrical equipment overturned and sank in the middle of the Clarence River and everything was lost. Or when he arrived in a town with his company only to find that the wagons containing all the equipment had been held up miles away by a flash flood.

McKay faced the problem with typical straightforwardness: told a huge audience waiting in the open air at eight o'clock that night what had happened, offered them their money back or a long wait until the gear arrived and the show could start. Nobody moved. The members of the company entertained the crowd with recitations and music until after midnight; then the wagons arrived, the tent was hastily erected, the audience filled it and the show began. When it finished in the early hours the audience rose to its feet and saluted McKay and his performers with 'For They Are Jolly Good Fellows'.

Such was the kind of respect McKay commanded wherever he went. According to those who remember him he was a man who loved a challenge as much as he loved show business. He had only one quirk: he never rode with the company when the show moved between adjacent towns; he walked instead, sometimes up to twenty miles. Irene Nelson says, 'He was never mean, was especially courteous to women and never uttered a "cuss" word.'

I met Stanley McKay in 1966 when he was eighty-nine years old. He had been retired for only four years and a short time before had been given a civic reception by the people of Rockhampton in recognition of his long service to country entertainment. I found him to be a sharp-witted, cheerful old gentleman. He told me why he had taken to the roads with a tent, and more about some of the problems he had faced while doing it.

'When I started in 1908 there were no theatres in New South Wales rural districts or anywhere outside Sydney barring the Victoria Theatre in Newcastle and the Civic Theatre in Bathurst. Both had dress circles, stalls and stage appointments, but the halls in New South Wales on the other hand were in a terrible state . . . small, badly lit and the seating was awful . . . about a hundred chairs and hardback forms, so it wasn't very exciting for people to come out and see shows then.

About that time—1908—and a few years later I took my company up the north coast. There were no trains in those days past Dungog so the company travelled by coach. Mine was a moving theatre, that is a tent theatre that held about a thousand people. It was carted from town to town by bullock team from Kempsey up to Grafton and so on.

The shows were varied. I had twenty-two people in my pantomime company, but when I presented comedy or drama I had only a dozen.

Some scenes in my presentations were lavish. For instance, when we played in the big tent I had a race scene from Nat Gould's racing drama, *The Double Event* using real horses, but I had a terrible experience at Kempsey. The night before it was due to go on for the first time, we presented a comedy called, *The Private Secretary* and when it was over I took a curtain call with the actors and told the audience—the tent was packed—about the show the following night. I made a big song and dance about it. I said, "We're going to present *The Double Event* in a manner which could not be handled in any city theatre, because we'll use real racehorses." Everybody was impressed.

Well, I had a scene painted showing the winning post of the

Melbourne Cup erected at the back of the stage, and I'd arranged for four horses to be supplied by a local livery stable. However, when I sent Props down to get them after the second act, he came back in a terrible stew saying the stables were locked up and the groom hadn't left the key!

What could I do? A full house and everybody waiting for the big scene, but no horses! Interval came and I walked down the side of the tent and on to the main street of Kempsey in extremis.

Then I saw three young fellows on horses. They were jogging back home to their farms. I hailed them and after I had told them my tale of woe, they said, "All right . . . we'll help you, mate." I said, "Right. Let me have your horses and come in and see one of them win the Melbourne Cup."

It worked, too. The scene sent the audience wild but nobody knew what a narrow escape I'd had . . . nobody could guess how scared and desperate I was until those young fellows came along the main street on their horses.

Once I was presenting a show in Molong, New South Wales and a well-known man in the town had just died. It was in 1923 and at the time I had a bellringer who used to go around the town spruiking and ringing his bell. He wasn't too bright and I impressed on him the need to be a bit quieter than usual. "Don't ring the bell out of sympathy for the relatives of the deceased," I told him.

Well he went out and I heard him yelling, "I want you all to come and see the big show tonight—" and he added "—yes, all of you, barring the deceased, of course." His humour wasn't well received, I can tell you. Ha ha—'

Henry Stanley McKay died in September 1971, just two weeks short of his ninety-seventh birthday.

Mrs Short, spruiker

I heard it first at Sydney's Royal Easter Show in 1959, a leathery voice, loud and commanding yelling 'Hurry! Hurry! Hurry!' It competed easily with the usual mix of musical mayhem in Sideshow Alley and I found it belonged to old Mrs Short, the grand duchess of Australia's women spruikers. With stick in hand, she had been walking up and down on the narrow boardwalk outside her tent on showgrounds all over Australia for more than sixty years, was one of a select band of travelling showfolk who cajoled the gullible to part with their money and see the wonders of the world awaiting them 'on the inside'.

When I talked with her about the 'attractions' and claimed that in the old days, many of them were simply cons she wouldn't agree, but enjoyed loudly describing some of them.

'For instance, we had an act with a horse; we told the customers that its head was where its tail should be and its tail was where its head should be. When they paid and walked into the marquee all they saw was a horse turned around with its tail in a feeding box.

Then there was the dancing duck. Not a bad idea that, because during a depression we were always sure of a good feed. We could eat the leading lady.

We placed the duck on a sheet of tin, and unknown to the audience there were two or three lighted candles underneath. When the tin got warm it danced better and better and it intrigued the children very much.

In my long experience, the biggest money-spinners in the tent-show business were the illusions. People loved to be fooled. They knew it was an illusion but they came back again and again, trying to find out how each was done. The laughing head on the sword, for instance. They used to shout, "It's all done with mirrors," but when they were invited up on the stage to have a look for themselves, they couldn't find any. And other illusions like The Guillotine, The Floating Lady and The Burning of She, all gave us a good living. These days freak shows such as The Pinheaded Chinaman are not allowed.

I first learned to spruik with Anna Polina my German strong girl . . . imported from Germany. She was amazing. She used to bend six-inch nails with her fingers, iron bars across every part of her body and using her teeth withdraw nails which had been hammered into wood by the audience . . . and right before your very eyes!

Without consciously doing so, Mrs Short was moving into her spruiking mode, and from habit talking as if to an invisible audience.

'In those days, ladies and gentlemen, you had to really entertain the public, and spruikers were the mainspring of the shows. They bellowed with their gravel voices; today nobody can spruik like them; they are a dying race. I spruiked with a tin horn . . . no microphones in those days. I have travelled the length and breadth of Australia . . . lived in tents, in little huts and whirlies like the blackfellows, any place where we could find shelter but the great days of travelling show business which the old timers talk about were before radio and television.'

She lowered her head as if to observe two minutes silence, and being wise in the dramatic and self-indulgent ways of performers I hastily headed her off with a tentative, 'Perhaps you could give me a sample of your spruiking technique—'

She needed no second invitation, and rendered a deafening 'Hurry . . . Hurry . . . Hurry! Step up! Step up—' and went on for a minute.

To my surprise people were lining up at the ticket box already, money in hand . . .

Dante, illusionist

Dante is a great name for an illusionist and apparently a common one; a number of them have performed in Australia during the past one hundred years. I met one in the 1960s—a dapper little elderly man in a black suit—and with his snow-white hair and Van Dyke beard he filled the part exactly.

'I made my first appearance as an illusionist at the Princess Theatre, Sydney on 8 October 1898, and later toured America then Australia. It became a regular tour and I did it many times after that.

Early on, I realised that people found it difficult to remember my name which was foreign, and Dante was suggested by a theatre manager who said, "You perform an illusion which has to do with cremation. Why not call yourself Dante after Dante's *Inferno*?" I did and I've performed under that name for the past seventy years.

My most famous trick? It is one I am pleased to call Madame Chang. To describe it precisely: on stage is a lion's cage, six feet high with steel bars all round. A young woman wearing a distinctive frock is placed inside it and a curtain is lowered halfway down, yet she is visible to the audience all the time. Next, the cage is hoisted up clear of the stage and on a word of command the young woman vanishes before your very eyes. Almost immediately, it seems the young woman reappears at the back of the stalls holding aloft some article, like a handkerchief which had been previously provided by a member of the audience.

That was my best illusion and so far I have never seen it duplicated. I was the only magician in the world who could do it. I was twenty-five at the time; it took me a year to perfect and it created a furore whenever and wherever I presented it.

I've had some funny experiences as an illusionist. In 1912 I was appearing in a Victorian theatre after a group of acrobats. As part of their presentation they required various trapdoors in different parts of the stage.

When they had finished their act, the band played my opening music and I made my entrance down a flight of stairs. It was very dignified and majestic. I reached the bottom, handed my red-lined cloak and cane to an assistant at the foot, took one step forward and promptly disappeared through a trap which somebody had forgotten to lock. I fell some distance in the dark on to a mattress which luckily somebody had forgotten to remove.

I jumped up, sprinted up a circular staircase and made a second entrance from the wings, to great applause from the audience who thought it was part of the act!

The theatre manager, who had seen it all, liked it and said, "You must leave that bit in," but I told him in no uncertain terms what I thought of him and the theatre, too!

Soon after that I toured New South Wales and at one theatre really needed a trapdoor for one of my illusions. I was provided with one, a cabinet would be placed over the trap, a woman assistant placed inside it, the door padlocked and after much wand-waving from me, she would vanish . . . through the trapdoor, of course. That was how it was supposed to be done but on the night, my regular assistant was unwell and after discreet enquiries I hired a local young lady who could be depended on not to tell everybody afterwards how the trick was done.

She was placed inside the cabinet, the door was padlocked and I proceeded blithely with the trick, but a mechanist watching from the wings somewhere behind me could see something at the back of the cabinet that I couldn't: she had become stuck half inside the trapdoor and half out of it and despite her struggles couldn't move an inch! Luckily, he showed great presence of mind, drew the tabs up to each side of the cabinet, rushed out behind them, gave her a hearty push and she fell through.

Afterwards I realised that I had picked the wrong girl, possibly because I was attracted by her fulsome figure. Her big bust was the trouble; it couldn't go through the trap without assistance!

I'm still working at eighty-one. The theatre these days is full of young people; it keeps me young, too. I feel as fit today as I did when I was thirty. Are illusionists as popular as they were? I think so. Every year there's a new generation and they're as prepared to accept such entertainment as avidly as they did fifty years ago.

I'm quite an old man now, yet despite the few years left to me I don't feel old by any means. I'm sure the greatest trick is yet to come.'

The Sydney Tivoli

The seedy old theatre had once been called the Sydney Opera House, but it had fallen on hard times, was 'dark' as they say in the profession, and in 1931 it was taken over by two vaudevillians, Mike Connors and his wife Queenie Paul in partnership with an entrepreneur, Neil Maver. They christened it The New Tivoli and their aim was to revive vaudeville.

Over the next thirty-five years they and other managements did just that.

There was nothing subtle about vaudeville at the Sydney Tiv. Its recipe for success was simple: a long line of shapely ballet girls, a smaller number of beautiful long-legged showgirls, numerous variety artists, both imported and homegrown, and a team of uproariously-funny comedians whose names belong to Australian theatrical history: Roy Rene ('Mo McCackie'), George 'Unkus' Wallace, Jim Gerald and many lesser lights who graced the stage, plied their trade and left them laughing.

Usually, there were two shows a day—except Sundays—a change of show every five weeks, and nothing at the Tiv strained the intellect. If a feed in a comedy sketch spouted an unfamiliar word of more than one syllable, George Wallace was apt to stop the action, look at the offender belligerently and say, 'You'll fry a hot sausage on my *what*?'

Or if Mo uttered a line of suggestive innuendo and cleaned it up with his hypocritical 'I hate anything coarse!' followed by a dirty leer, the Tivoli audience got the message and was devastated.

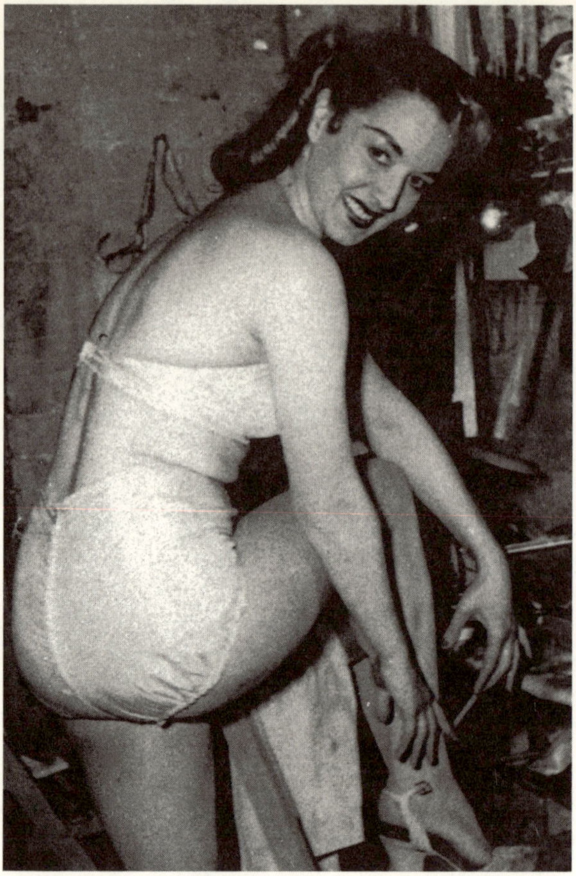

'. . . beautiful, long-legged showgirls . . .'

And from the day the Tivoli opened its doors, it was mecca for every stagestruck kid who ever learned dancing, her dream to be auditioned and accepted for a lowly-paid job in the famous Tivoli ballet.

Ronnie Hay, the Tiv's ballet master, choreographer and set designer calculated that he taught two thousand ballet dancers during his twenty-two years at the Tiv. And surprisingly, many of the 'girls' who live in Sydney still keep in touch, get together regularly, and thumbing their noses at the passing of time and aching muscles don their dancing shoes and tap to recorded music once a fortnight. Mercia George, a former ballet girl said:

'I started at the Tiv in 1929 as a dancer in a line of sixteen ballet girls. I worked on stage solidly for the next ten years, then I started to teach dancing in Maurice Diamond's School of Dancing which was situated at the top of the gallery stairs. I did that until the Tiv closed in 1966 and I had to teach elsewhere.

In the late 1920s and 1930s we worked very hard . . . the dancing was strenuous. We did as many as eight routines in a single show, danced up and down stairs, made quick changes, and apart from that rehearsed every morning from ten-thirty until one o'clock, preparing for the next production. One way and another we spent our lives in the theatre; we weren't allowed to go outside, even with a coat over our costumes to buy a sandwich from a shop nearby!

But it was a healthy life with so much exercise and one had to be strong to do it; the average age of dancers was between sixteen and twenty-five. Not much chance of getting fat. However, if anybody put on an extra pound or two, she was handed a diet sheet by the management!'

Another ballet girl, Lorraine Forbes remembers attending an audition for dancers at the Tiv in 1945:

'A friend of mine was auditioning and I went along to keep her company. She was unsuccessful, then the producer, Ginger James saw me sitting down in the stalls, and asked if I could dance. My friend, who was a good sport gave me a wrap up, explained that I had attended the same dancing school as herself. Mr James invited me up on the stage, I danced a little, he looked me over and a few days later I got a telegram telling me I had the job. What a thrill it was! I stayed with the Tiv ballet for three years.

There was only one hiccup. Soon after I joined I was told that in the next show the girls had to dance topless. I didn't want to and was upset about it. David N. Martin, the big boss of the Tivoli circuit asked me what was the matter and when I told him, he said, "Don't worry about it. You can skip this show and come back to work in the next one." I thought it was very sweet of him, but that kind of thing was not unusual at the Tiv. As far as the ballet girls were concerned we were like a big family.'

Former dancer Dorothy Davey recalls:

'Being a Tivoli ballet girl carried a lot of prestige in the 1930s and 1940s. It was thought to be glamorous, a bit like being a air hostess when flying came in later on.'

Len James was a member of the Tivoli orchestra for a large part of his life. Previously, he had been with George Sorlie's tent shows for some years, moving weekly from one New South Wales country town to the next, then in the late 1930s he was invited to audition for the position of pianist at the Tiv.

'I got the job, and I couldn't believe my good luck. I considered it as the peak of my career. After five years the management tried me out as deputy conductor. Later I graduated as conductor and held that post until the theatre closed.

I conducted for nearly every local and overseas artist who appeared on the Tivoli circuit in Sydney, Melbourne and Adelaide. Some weren't so popular with audiences. Like George Formby, for instance. All he did was perform the songs we had heard on the radio. The famous English music hall artist George Robey failed because he was too "blue", Stanley Holloway with his poems like "Sam Pick Up Thy Musket" didn't go down well, either.

I remember the first time Shirley Bassey came to Australia under contract to the Tivoli. Everybody in the orchestra was agog and we looked forward to meeting her at rehearsal time. Her music was handed down to us early in the morning and we decided to get the arrangement down pat before she arrived, so we played it over a few times.

Then I looked up and saw a little lady with no shoes on, who had come on while we were playing and now was sitting with her legs dangling over the footlights.

We finished playing and I said, "Good morning, Miss Bassey."

She replied, "Yeah, and what was *that* you were playing?"

"Your opening number," I said.

She said, "It sounded like nothin'."

Later though, we found she was a delight to work with.

There was often a lot of pressure during performances at the Tiv, and some mishaps which were very funny.

I remember a first night when everybody was working against the clock. Mechanists and technicians were completing the set for the opening scene right up until curtain time. They had built three huge shells, each to contain a showgirl. They finished just on eight o'clock, the girls rushed on to take their places and after some confusion, the shells were closed, the curtain rose and they were on. However, when the shells opened there were girls in only two of them. A carpenter in overalls with a hammer in his hand was in the third. He hurried off the stage very embarrassed.

One of the oddest experiences I had conducting the Tiv orchestra was with the girl who was the original voice for Disney's "Snow White and the Seven Dwarfs". She sounded lovely but it was the smallest voice I ever heard. She appeared on stage in a garden setting and there were trees and flowers everywhere, with a concealed microphone behind each. One night they failed and I can still see the poor girl, running from flower to flower trying to find one that worked.'

Mercia George said:

'It's generally believed that with all the stage lighting performers can't see much of the audience, but at the Tiv we could see all the way, almost to the back of the stalls and it was terrific to be on stage when the curtain rose at eight o'clock to find yourself staring at a packed house.

I'll never forget what happened one afternoon, though. There was a club-swinging routine in the show, and unlike the other girls I wasn't very good at it so the choreographer put me in the back line for a while. I must have got used to the club swinging because I was repositioned in the front after a week or so but on this terrible afternoon I was swinging my club and, brother, I accidentally let it go!

It went out over the orchestra pit straight for an elderly gentleman sitting in the front row. It hit him on the head and he fell out of his seat! The conductor looked round, saw what had happened, patted him on the head reassuringly with his free hand and asked if he was all right. The old chap nodded, picked up my club, handed it to the conductor who threw it back to me over the footlights. He hadn't missed a beat! The old chap sat through the rest of the show so he must have been all right.'

Backstage, the Tivoli Theatre was a rabbit warren of passages, dressing rooms and offices, dark and pervaded by the smells of makeup, dust and freshly painted scenery. Like many old theatres it gave the impression that so much energy had been expended in creating the glitz and gaudy make-believe on stage that not enough had been left over to tidy up the real world behind.

Then one evening in September 1945 the two almost became one. A ballet girl, Joyce Smith, then twenty years old (now sixty-seven) remembers vividly what happened:

'It was twenty past nine on a Thursday night. I was in the dressing room on the first floor with seven other ballet girls and we had just been told by the callboy that we had five minutes before our next number.

Everything was quiet, as it usually was backstage, then I heard terrible screams from upstairs on the second floor where the showgirls had their dressing room. I rushed out to see what had happened. There was smoke everywhere and one of the showgirls was on fire! She was running all over the landing in a panic, and tried to jump over a railing on to the stage, fifty feet below. Two other showgirls were on fire, too. Terrible confusion . . . people running everywhere . . . yelling and trying to help. A chorus boy grabbed the first girl just in time and rolled her on the floor and put out the flames. Somebody rang the ambulance and fire brigade. Then the automatic sprinklers started to work and we were all soaked with water.

Then the three showgirls were carried down and laid on the landing outside our dressing room. They were terribly burnt. One of them, Phyllis Haines, poor kid, was only fifteen. We got dressing-gowns and covered them up until the ambulances came.'

Joyce Smith, Tiv ballet (left) and Joyce Smith, today

Comedian Roy Rene ('Mo') was in his dressing room with his wife, Sadie Gale, preparing for his next appearance at the time of the fire, and Sadie remembers:

'Roy was having trouble with his dentures. He had a sore mouth and had taken them out for a while and put them on top of a wardrobe. When we saw all the smoke and realised that there was a fire he panicked. "Gawd!" he said. "Me tatts . . . the bloody tatts . . . where are they?" They were his first thought.'

Len James was conducting the orchestra in the pit:

'The house was packed and we had just started the second half. Then I heard the alarm bells ringing faintly backstage. About the same time I noticed some smoke above the audience. I looked down and saw that water was starting to rise in the pit and it was over the soles of my shoes.

I knew by now, of course that there must have been a fire in the theatre and that the basement had filled with water already. I could see that the rest of the orchestra were aware of it too but we kept on going.'

Meanwhile, backstage, Roy Rene had found his teeth, put them in and Sadie says 'he ran down through the smoke to the wings and waited, ready to go on and ad lib should the fire spread and the audience panic'.

However, by now the fire brigade and ambulances had arrived; the fire which had not spread far had been brought under control; and the three showgirls, all badly burned had been taken to hospital.

Joyce Smith takes up the story:

'We were told what had happened. Phyllis Haynes had just changed into her next costume, a black velvet top and a pink net skirt with only a bra and G-string underneath, and she was running out of the dressing room when her skirt brushed against a radiator and caught alight. Two other showgirls, Diana Hart and Jean McKenzie ran to help her and their costumes, which were the same, caught alight, too.

We were all terribly upset, but Queenie Paul, the producer got us together, talked to us then shepherded us downstairs and into position ready to go on with our next routine.

It was a perfect example of the old saying "the show must go on". We continued playing right up until the end of the show at eleven o'clock, despite the fact that a couple of the ballet girls fainted on stage and were hurried off. Then the audience left, completely unaware of the terrible happenings backstage. Altogether, it was my saddest experience in the theatre.'

(Tragically, as a result of the fire, one of the showgirls, Jean McKenzie died in hospital. A few days later, the Tivoli ballet girls attended her funeral.)

'Afterwards we returned to the Tiv for the evening performance. We felt terribly down and dreaded it but worse was to come. When we arrived at the stage door we were told that Phyllis Haines, the fifteen-year-old had just died also.

Diana Hart, who had also been badly burned spent nine months in hospital. She was scarred for life.'

The Tivoli comedians

Roy Rene (Mo)

For more than thirty years, Harry van der Sluice or simply 'Mo McCackie', a spluttering Jewish comedian was top of the bill at Tivoli theatres in Sydney, Melbourne and Adelaide.

He was a natural. Born of theatrical parents in 1892, his first role on stage—prophetically—was in comedy. He played the back part of a duck at the age of eight.

Later, as a boy soprano he earned £3 a week at Melbourne's Gaiety Theatre. As a young man he was cornerman in black minstrel shows, then in 1914, Nat Phillips an American comedian came to Australia, saw Roy working and teamed up with him in comedy sketches and a famous theatrical team, 'Stiffy and Mo' was born.

They worked together at the old Princess Theatre in Railway Square, Sydney until Stiffy died in 1936. Then Roy Rene, on his own and using the stark black and white makeup of earlier minstrel shows to his comic advantage combined with a unique kind of Jewish humour became 'Mo McCackie', and before long his lisping, supercilious, rather wet delivery made him the most popular standup comic in Australia.

On stage, Roy could reduce a conservative audience to near hysteria with a line, a confidential aside, a gesture or a mincing walk down to the footlights to deliver a familiar line like, 'I was about as popular as a ham sandwich at a Jew's picnic!' He was one of the greats of vaudeville.

Roy Rene ('Mo McCackie') (left) and Roy Rene offstage. He was a natty dresser

His widow and frequent partner in sketches on stage, Sadie Gale, now living in a Sydney nursing home says, 'He lived for the stage and the audience, and was unhappy away from them. It was his life.'

Len James said, 'Roy Rene was the funniest comedian I ever worked with. I never tired of watching him, yet offstage he was dour and very hard to get a laugh out of. He wasn't exactly lavish in his praise of other performers either. I remember when Larry Adler, the famous mouth organ virtuoso was rehearsing at the Tiv, and Roy and I were watching him from the wings.

I asked, 'What do you think of him, Roy?'

'Not much,' Roy said with a sniff. 'I mean . . . take away the bugger's mouth organ and what has he got?'

James was quick to add though that Roy was not above playing a theatrical joke or two. He remembered one of the bit players in Roy's sketches, who, no matter what kind of part he played always liked to wear a false moustache. Bearing this in mind, Roy crept into his dressing room before a performance one evening and mixed some ground-up gorgonzola cheese with the spirit gum which the actor used to hold his moustache in place. During the show Roy circled the man more than once saying 'You smell funny, pal!' No

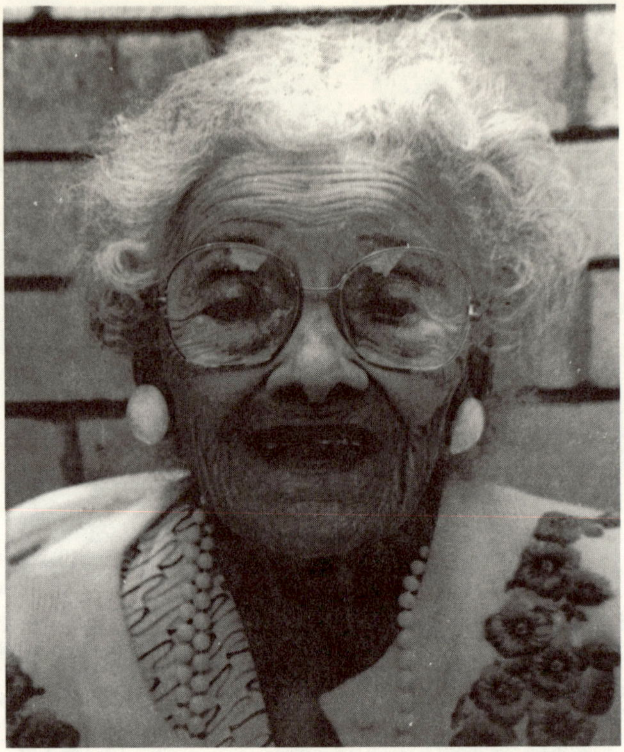

Sadie Gale, today

doubt the actor, with the moustache and the spirit gum under his nose agreed.

In the 1940s Roy was persuaded to make a film. It was called *Strike It Lucky* but it didn't do him justice. He appeared lost without a live audience to complement his instinctive timing. He was more successful with a gramophone record which was released about the same time. Called 'Are you all right, lovey?' it was a sketch with Roy Rene, Sadie Gale and company. The plot was simple enough: Mo and his 'lovey' on their honeymoon stayed at an expensive hotel and when a bill was presented to them by the manager for expensive meals they hadn't eaten, Mo was outraged.

MO:	It's absolutely abdominal! Poor Florrie here has hardly eaten a caraway seed. We didn't eat all that—
MANAGER:	Well, it was there if you wanted it.
MO:	All right. I charge you a hundred pounds for kissing my wife!
MANAGER:	I didn't kiss your wife.
MO:	Well, it was there if you wanted it!

Sadie Gale helps her husband Mo to dress for 'Elizabeth the Virgin Queen'

Roy received several tempting offers to work in America but he refused. 'Look what the Yanks did to Pharlap and Les Darcy,' he said. 'I don't want to make a treble. Not me, pal!'

Roy Rene as 'Elizabeth, the Virgin Queen', as 'Henry VIII', as 'Floating Flossie' (a mock levitation act) or reciting one of his greatest successes, 'The Green Eye of the Little Yellow God' will be remembered by oldsters who enjoyed outrageous 'Mo' and were cheered by his familiar catchcries: 'Strike me lucky!', 'The dirty mug!' and 'Curse my fatal beauty!'

Or they may recall a sketch in which Mo pawned his overcoat and got a measly five bob for it. 'Daylight robbery,' he complained. 'Why, the beer in the lapels was worth more than that!' He shivered without his overcoat, and moaned, 'It's cold enough to—' At that moment three brass balls above the pawnbroker's door crashed to the stage. And in the 1940s, during his radio days his cry of 'Cop this, young 'arry!' followed by a whack, not to mention his timeless put down of all monologists: 'Flo-o-o-o's Letter!' were enough to bring his faithful audience back again and again.

Roy, who had gone on only two holidays in his life—he said he never liked to be far from the theatre—suffered a heart condition in the early 1950s and was forced to cut down on his stage appearances, but made big plans for working in television when it started in Australia.

For once his instinctive sense of timing failed him. He died in 1954, two years before it was introduced.

Jenny Howard

During a long career, Jenny Howard, the Tiv's most memorable comedienne headlined twenty-five shows on the Tivoli circuit, a record unequalled by any other comedienne.

She was an import. Born Daisy Evelyn Louise Bowes (a name too long, unfortunately for front-of-house advertising) at Walthamstowe, England in 1902 she made her debut on the stage at the age of twelve and graduated in vaudeville, pantos and musical revues. After several command performances, she was brought out to Australia under contract to appear at the Tivoli.

By now she was Jenny Howard, and had married Percy King who, apart from being her producer and manager was known in Sydney as an entrepreneur who brought African midgets to Sydney for sideshow appearances at the Easter Show.

Len James remembered:

'She was the most consistent and hardest-working entertainer I ever met and gave her all at every performance. She had a razor-sharp soprano voice and sang a lot in her act, and a funny thing happened one Saturday during a matinee. A plague of flying ants had got into the theatre and the air was thick with them. It was near the end of one of Jenny's numbers and she was about to take a top note. She drew breath and inhaled a mouthful of the things. The result was chaotic but the audience loved it; they thought it was part of the act.

And that wasn't the end of it. That evening, David N. Martin, the boss of the Tivoli circuit rang the Sydney manager from Melbourne as usual and asked how the shows had gone that day.

"Well, we had the flying ants in this afternoon," he told Martin. "They nearly caused a riot."

"The Flying Ants, eh?" Martin said. "Well, if they're that good, book them!"'

Jenny's most popular song was that old romantic pot boiler 'A Heart That's Free'. Sung in her ear-splitting soprano and accompanied by aerobic movements of the arms and body it could not be easily forgotten. A flautist provided an obligato and near the end of the number played several short phrases, each of which Jenny copied

Jenny Howard in a glamorous mood

with bell-like notes. However, each was half an octave higher than the last until finally the flautist let himself go with a long complicated bit ending on a note well above high C.

Jenny paused, said 'Not bloody likely!' and walked off to applause.

When she reached what is considered to be retiring age, Jenny reluctantly wound down her stage appearances, but drama—or was it tragi-comedy—hadn't finished with her yet.

She and her sister, Lily, were finishing lunch in the Bondi Diggers' Club one day in 1983 when a grey-haired man came up, made himself known and claimed that he had been a fan of Jenny's for many years. Jenny, an impressionable, generous soul was flattered, but sister Lily was suspicious and tried to discourage him.

She wasn't successful. The weather was bad and the man offered both a ride home in his car. Jenny accepted and when they got there she invited him in for a cup of tea. She was eighty-one and lonely, the man was sixty-nine and attentive and not surprisingly romance blossomed. Before long they got married and settled on the Gold Coast and her husband took charge of her affairs.

In 1985 one of Jenny's oldest friends, comedian Bobby Le Brun died in Newcastle and she and her husband drove down for the funeral. Then the unexpected. The husband suffered a stroke at the graveside, was taken to the hospital where Bobby Le Brun had died and died there himself.

(As irreverent Roy Rene might have said, 'The mug, doin' a thing like that at a funeral! He could have cast a pall of gloom over the whole proceedings!')

At the time of writing, Jenny Howard resides quietly at Burleigh Heads, Queensland. She is ninety.

George ('Unkus') Wallace

George Wallace was one of the funniest comedians Australia has produced. Roy Rene was more famous but the character he created was unique and resembled nobody, while Australian audiences recognised George at once as one of themselves.

He was the pot-bellied labourer dropping in at the pub for a drink after work with half-baked opinions on everything or the guy sitting next to you on the bus who insisted on chatting when you wanted to think or read your paper or the ill-informed interjector at public meetings. Like many of his kind in the 1920s and 1930s he was a leaner—liked to lean on something—he was as Australian as meat pies and bread-and-butter custard. His voice was a strong part of his act; it was gutteral, bubbled along, ignored full stops and you longed for him to have a good cough and clear his throat.

It was not generally known, but Wallace was an accomplished dancer. One of his favourite tricks was what he called 'A silly bugger's roll', a kind of tumble which he perfected himself. He would trip himself up, roll in the air and end up face down on the floor, a split second before he knocked himself out.

He rarely worked 'blue' on stage but at theatrical parties he was a riot and gained a reputation for one trick which, in more conservative circles might have resulted in female faintings, masculine threats or even arrest. In highly questionable taste it can be best described as one where he purported to be assisting in handing around hors d'ouevres to guests. The plate, held low, was suitably garnished with parsley, spring onions and bits of cheese and looked legitimate enough, but the centrepiece, of no interest to vegetarians was part of George himself.

Women liked George. Mercia George knew him from the time she was a little girl and often in adulthood while working with him in sketches on stage he would try to break her up with wild departures from the script. She said, 'I would dry because I never knew what he would say or what I was supposed to say next. It was terrifying!'

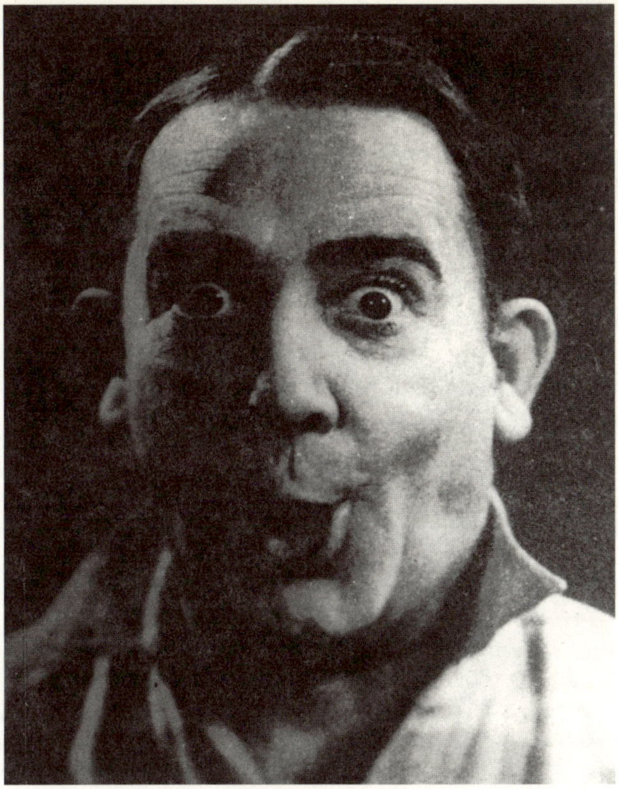

George ('Unkus') Wallace

Like Roy Rene, George was a painter of some ability and former ballet girl, Irene Nelson still regrets that despite numerous promises he never gave her one of his pictures.

Virginia Ransom, a Sydney fashion consultant who had only heard of George as a child was luckier. A short time ago, searching for a picture frame in a Newtown second-hand shop she found one with a painting in it already. It was inscribed 'To Frank and Piri. From George Wallace. Melbourne 1957'.

The dealer, a foreigner who obviously had never heard of George Wallace sold her the lot for $35 and the painting in its frame now occupies pride of place on a wall in her flat. It's not a Rembrandt or a Streeton but, like George, has a charm of its own.

In the early 1960s when George's career—and his life—were drawing to a close, he starred in a nostalgic revue with other veterans of vaudeville called 'The Good Old Days', first at the Paris Theatre then at Sydney's Theatre Royal.

By now he had become so blasé, he would arrive at the Paris just before his act, walk on without makeup, convulse the audience then walk off and go home. Sometimes, he didn't even take off his overcoat!

However, when the show moved to the Royal he did a hilarious piece called 'Sophie the Sort on the Bus' and it demanded more preparation. Written by George in the 1950s, 'Sophie' was born when the New South Wales Transport Department took a revolutionary step and recruited women conductors for Sydney buses.

It didn't take long for the conductresses in their ill-fitting uniforms to become the butt of local humour. George Wallace saw the opportunities, too. He had already impersonated a busty lady bowler with his 'Queen of the Bowling Green' and now he came up with Sophie. His impersonation of a Sydney bus conductress in a navy blue uniform, a long daggy black wig, money bag and black stockings was wickedly accurate. Only his gravel voice remained the same—apart from a suggestion here and there of mock upper-class gentility—and he didn't smile once.

SOPHIE THE SORT ON THE BUS

SCENE: THE BACK OF A DOUBLE-DECKER BUS

(Passengers are alighting, shaking their heads and talking among themselves).

INDIGNANT WOMAN: —and you know what?
MAN: What?
INDIGNANT WOMAN: (LOUDLY) She wanted to toss me double or quits for the change. I think she is the most nauseating woman I have ever m—

(George appears and leaves the bus. He is dressed in the blue conductress's uniform familiar to all Sydneysiders, with tickets and change in a bag around his neck. He wears a long-haired black wig and there all femininity ends. His gravelly voice is unchanged.)

GEORGE: I heard every word you said. How dare you speak about me behind my bus!
WOMAN: I've got my rights on a public bus. I paid my fare I did and—
GEORGE: You'll get a smack in the mouth with the day's takings if you're not careful. Next time they have a flood down the River Murray why don't you go down there?
WOMAN: (STILL YELLING) Why should I go down the River Murray next time they have a flood?
GEORGE: They want all the bags they can get!
WOMAN: (SCREAMS) I tell you—
GEORGE: Now look love run away and collide with yourself.
WOMAN: How dare you! I am NOT a bag.

GEORGE: You are. You are the original Miss Hessian. Go away—
WOMAN: I am not a bag. (GRANDLY) I am a singer.
GEORGE: So is our sewing machine . . .

Orchestra strikes up: Passengers exit: George comes downstage

GEORGE: (SINGS) I was as happy as I could bee, packin' pickles in the factoree,
One fine morning without any fuss, I went and I got me, a job on a bus.
(CHORUS) Oh, I'm Sophie the sort, the extra good sort,
Sophie the sort on the bus,
Punching the tickets, young and carefree
Dead lairs and lovers get attention from me
I'm used to the swanks, the drunks and the Yanks,
Carefree, I don't give a cuss,
I never get excited when the horn starts to honk,
I'll be in a bit of nonsense and I love a drop of plonk.
With girls it ever was thus
I'm Sophie the sort on the —

(SPEAKS) You've no idea what we women have to put up with on these buses. You wouldn't have the faintest conception. And it's the women. I hate talking about my own sex but my Gawd, it's the women. For example that one there. You know what's the matter with her, don't you? She started out to be an old maid but she couldn't stick to the rules!

I'm not a woman to talk but the buses are driving me mad. Me nerves are shattered. Just a bundle of nerves that's all. I used to have a lovely nature once. Now I do me block at the drop of a hat. I dunno.

The other day . . . last Tuesday . . . no Wednesday a man got on the bus with a dog . . . the biggest dog you have ever seen in your life! A dirty big heifer, er, a mastiff and they walked on to the bus, the man and the dog, went over and sat on a seat together. I was aghast. *I was aghast*!

I let them sit there for about five minutes, then I went over and in a ladylike voice said, 'Look, what the bloody—' I said, 'Look, you can't have the dog on the seat! He said, 'Now then my sweet little girl—' and I said, 'Sarcasm won't get you anywhere! Under the shop assistants' award you can't have the dog on the bus. Get off!'

Well, he took the dog and got off the bus, then he turned very nasty and very dirty. You wouldn't read about what he said. He didn't whisper it; he screamed it out like a mad black; you could hear him everywhere. You know what he said, don't you? He looked me straight in the ball of the eye and he said, 'You know what you can do with your bus, don't you?'

I said, 'You do the same thing with your dog and you can get back on the bus!'

I'm a girl, you know who loves refinement. (Adopts a phony upper-class accent.) Culture, the arts and music. I like to speak like a lady, and do and say the things a lady would do and say. (Becomes his common self.)

I'm having a stink with a sheila in a fish shop and she's buying a bit of mullet . . . a ninepenny bit with the gills in. Well, one word led to another and she let go. Now I don't know whether you've ever been smacked in the mouth with a bit of fried mullet . . . with the gills in, but it's a nauseating experience and it's an each-way bet which gill the fat's goin' to squirt out of first.

Well, I realised that breeding was definitely out. I said, 'Fiddle-de-dee' and went to sweep regally out of the fish shop, but some *galah* had left half a frankfurt on the floor. I skidded on that, bashed the base of me skull on the iron railing of the counter, me right hand went in the batter fat and I finished up in a mangled heap on a bag of prawns . . . eight-and-six a pound!

I was laying there, unconscious in a stumor and this is where my mad Latin lover comes into the story: Ginger Ferguson. There's a nice animal for you! Thinks he's engaged to me. Ha! Ha! Ha! That'll be the day. Oh no, he wants all his own way.

When I came out of the stumor Ginger was holding me up. He looked me straight in the face with his one good eye and then he asked me to go out with him. Well you know when they ask you to go out with them you feel as silly as a duck and don't know what to say. I said, 'Maybe I will and maybe I won't.' I can't make me mind up and I'm dying to go with him all the time! Well, I went out with him, but my Gawd, never again! Aw no . . fair's fair. I learned more wrestling grips in a quarter of an hour . . . next day I went to help an old bloke on to the bus and I broke his back in three places.

He's mad, that Ginger Ferguson . . . mad as a snake. I thought he was a normal kind of feller but he's a raving ratbag. You wouldn't read about the things he does. I was going to a square dance with him and I had a lovely dress made. They reckoned I looked almost human and you know what he did? Pinched me powder compact, took the face powder out and put self-raising flour in. It was a hot night and before the dance I went into the girls' room to powder off a bit. Halfway through the dance, what happened? I broke out in a batch of bloody scones! Walking around the room with knobs on!

It was in the country, I went out a side door to get a breath of fresh air and bumped into a tall woman with long black hair. I said, 'I'm awfully sorry, Madam. Pardon' and found I was talking to the back of a horse. My landlady, Mrs Drag . . . she's the one you don't know whether she's with you or at you. She said to me, 'Sophie, that old sofa in your room. I think I'll get it recovered. What colour would you like?'

I got a bit coy and carried away and said, 'I'd like it the same colour as my eyes.'

She said, 'Whoever heard of a bloodshot sofa?'

GEORGE: (SINGS) Oh I'm used to the swanks, the drunks and the Yanks,
Carefree, I don't give a cuss,
When my work is over and I'm liable to roam,
The policeman looks at me and he says, 'Lassie, go home',
With us girls it ever was thus,
I'm Sophie the sort on the bus, that's me,
Sophie, the sort on the—

(He walks off to thunderous applause without finishing the song).

George Wallace died in 1968. A few months before the end, my comedy-writing collaborator, the late George Foster, with whom Wallace appeared in radio's 'Bunkhouse Show' for some years paid him a visit to find out how he was getting on. He found Wallace seated at a table in the kitchen of his modest flat. In front of him were five screw-topped jam jars and in each was a spider. George was talking to them, addressing each by a pet name . . .

George Foster's experience set me thinking about other comics.

One, whose name I can't remember never went anywhere without his pet mice; Roy Rene couldn't eat a thing before a performance—his mouth was too dry—and he was always on edge until he got his first laugh; and then there was Will Mahoney, husband of Evie Hayes who made her name in the late 1940s with 'Annie Get Your Gun'. Willie, who she called 'her little mannie' was famed, not only as a standup comic, but because he was thought to be the only performer in the world who could stand on his head and play a xylophone with his feet. I met him for the first time at the Melbourne Tivoli in 1940 and was amazed to find that he was building a large boat backstage and was working on it during the show. What's more the Tivoli management encouraged him to do so. Willy was an alcoholic and management found that allowing him to pursue his hobby at the theatre was the only way to keep him off the booze between appearances.

Funny people, comedians.

Whatever happened to vaudeville with its earthy comedy and overdrawn characters, its dancers and showgirls, its unending variety, and the patrons out front who knew that vaudeville could always be depended on for a good night out?

Part of it died at the Sydney Tiv one evening in 1966. At the end of the show, the stage manager, Durham Marcel should have called, 'Stand by the act drop . . . lower the act drop in!' but he was silent, the main curtain stayed up and the cast simply walked off the stage.

'I'm not going to put the lid on the coffin!' he yelled.

It was more than the end of a performance; after thirty-five laughter-filled years, it was the last show at the Sydney Tiv. Audiences for vaudeville had dwindled and developers were waiting to move in, yet the theatre was dark for nearly three years before it was torn down and replaced with a box-like office block to house government departments.

Today, twenty-five years after, Durham Marcel is still angry.

'They're always complaining that Sydney doesn't have a theatre big enough for productions like "Phantom Of The Opera".' he says. 'The Tivoli could have done it, with two thousand seats, its enormous stage and with every facility backstage for producing the biggest shows in the business!'

There was no wake for the Tivoli in 1966, nothing done to mark its demise. Sadie Gale says, 'Whenever I'm driven past there today, I turn my head away. I don't want to see what's on the spot where the Tivoli stood.'

Unfortunately, the Tiv, like all live theatres depended for its success on the chancy stuff that dreams are made of, the kind of make-believe that doesn't stand a chance against the hardheaded world of commerce and changing times.

Sorry, Marcel . . . . sorry, Sadie. That's showbiz!

Hi Ho and Howdy!

No look back on entertainers of the past in Australia would be complete without a candid appraisal of two of the most famous: Bob Dyer and Jack Davey. For almost a quarter of a century they were at the top of the heap in commercial radio, their shows heard in most Australian households four and sometimes five nights a week.

I worked with both for many years as a comedy writer, ideas man and performer. I was also their friend.

Their paths to success were markedly different. In 1932, Jack Davey, then twenty-eight, a window dresser and part-time radio announcer in New Zealand decided to try his luck in Australian radio. After a bumpy start and numerous auditions he got himself a job as a breakfast announcer with station 2GB Sydney.

Bob Dyer (or 'Dyes', his correct name) was born and raised in Tennessee, USA and appeared in travelling revues before he came to Australia with an all-American production, *The Marcus Show* in 1937. A hillbilly comic, he wore a tight coat, shortish pants, a porkpie hat, played the ukulele and mouth organ (often at the same time) and sang raucous hillbilly songs like 'The Martins and the Coys' ('they were reckless mountain boys') and 'The Death of Willie' (who 'died, blew his nose and died again'). His voice was high, he giggled a lot and the tone of his act is best illustrated perhaps by a question from a regular stooge in the audience who, referring to Bob's 'yaller' boots yelled, 'Hey, were they always that colour, Bob or did you walk in something on the way over?'

In 1938 Dyer quit *The Marcus Show*, got work with the Tivoli circuit in Melbourne and attracted some publicity by wooing and marrying a beautiful Tivoli showgirl, Dolly Mack in nine days. Then he decided to try his luck in Australian radio. He was big, brash and pushy and it wasn't long before he won a contract with 3DB Melbourne to produce and star in two hillbilly shows, 'The Solvol Show' and 'You Ain't Heard Nuthin' Yet'.

By 1940 he found himself in need of a comedy writer, heard about me, arranged a meeting and within a short time I was hired to work with he and Dolly. They were great company and we became friends; however a year later, I was called up for the army. Before I left Bob insisted that we should keep in touch.

While this was going on, Jack Davey was on the move as well, expanding his interests at 2GB Sydney and already trying out some quiz ideas on local audiences.

Four years later, in 1945 I was still in the army and stationed at Lae, New Guinea. Bob who *had* kept in touch, and whose contribution to Australia's war effort so far had been unremarkable, decided that with the Japs on the run and the end of the war in sight, he and Dolly should take a concert party on a six-weeks tour of the northern battlefronts to entertain the troops.

When he arrived in Lae he sought me out and I wrote some topical material for his show. I remember only one of the gags and Bob used it that night before a huge forces audience. 'The troops up here will do anything to get home,' he yelled. 'Yesterday I saw a guy down at the water's edge. He had paddles on both feet, two more on his hands, and a sail on a mast in his mouth. I won't tell you where he had the outboard motor!'

It won a scream of approval from the troops and Bob wondered why. Much of his own material was 'blue' and was about husbands and wives having sex. It went down like a lead balloon with the troops most of whom had not seen their wives or sweethearts for more than a year, and their women were sacred to them. Chaplains who attended the show complained and Bob and his party left for other battlefronts in a hurry.

When the Japanese surrendered, I got a telegram from Bob: 'Won't be long now, pappy. [He called everybody 'pappy']. Contact me as soon as you get out.'

I did in 1946. After being demobbed I journeyed to Sydney where Bob had a contract with a national sponsor to produce and compere a radio show called 'Can You Take It?'. It was a copy of another in America called 'People are Funny' in which contestants were subjected to all kinds of indignities in return for big prizes. The sponsor signed me up for one year to write comedy and dream up stunts for CYTI. I arranged to bring my wife and child over as soon as I could find accommodation—it was scarce after the war—and in the meantime moved in and lived with Bob and Dolly at their home at Balmoral.

The author with Bob Dyer during 'Can You Take It?' production, 1948

Then the show began. Contestants were smacked in the face with meringue pies, doused with soda water and there was much mess and mayhem on the stage of the 2UW auditorium, to the accompaniment of Bob's familiar cry, 'Aren't we devils, customers?'

The radio audience loved it all. It was the right medicine after years of war, yet despite the big prizes, listeners were amazed at the gullibility of contestants, at their apparent willingness to be humiliated in public in such a radio program.

What they didn't know was that, 'Can You Take It?' was stooged up to the hilt; each stunt was almost choreographed to make sure that it worked and victims were put through their paces as carefully as performing animals in a circus.

Often, Bob and I picked up stooges on Saturday afternoons, a few hours before the broadcast, on Gowing's corner in Market Street near the theatre stage door, buttonholed them with 'How would you like to win £50 in a radio show tonight?' It was a considerable sum then and there were plenty of takers.

I was amazed that nobody suspected that 'Can You Take It?' was not the impromptu show it was supposed to be. Nobody, not even newspaper reporters went for the jugular with claims that Bob was conning the radio audience. Perhaps it was because he was such a superb showman, and was prepared to take risks. 'Can You Take It?' was broadcast live on fifty-two stations around Australia and sometimes, when despite careful preparation a stunt looked like collapsing, he could always get the show back on track. His size and massive self-confidence helped.

Probably, the best-known stunt we devised was one we called 'The Castlereagh Street Pram Push'. In theory, it seemed simple enough. The format: a male contestant would be 'chosen' from the studio audience and if he failed to answer a quiz question he would be invited to accept a challenge for £100, namely to dress up as a nursemaid and push a pram containing a midget (dressed as a baby) along Castlereagh Street in Sydney during the lunch hour a few days hence.

Bob realised that with the extra prize money and the likely publicity involved, he would need a stooge who could be depended on to keep his mouth shut. It was a problem. We looked around for some days and until only a few hours before the show, then we found one: Ray Mitchell, a young man who worked for the Mosman garage where Bob bought his petrol.

That evening, so that everybody in the studio audience would have an 'equal' chance of being selected for 'a special stunt' each person was given a ticket at the door; one half went into a box and the other half was retained. As soon as Ray Mitchell turned up however, his ticket number was noted and when everybody was seated, the box was taken backstage, the ticket butts thrown out and a new batch substituted, each with Mitchell's number on.

There was near-disaster though just before the broadcast when Bob invited an eleven-year-old boy up on stage to pull the 'winning' ticket from the box. Luckily, I was standing behind him as he put his hand in and I noted that he was palming his own ticket, held in place with his thumb. I wrenched it from him just in time, and Ray Mitchell, not by fair means but foul was 'chosen' as the contestant; was 'unable' to answer Bob's quiz question and on cue accepted his challenge to act as a nursemaid in Castlereagh Street for the sum of £100.

The stunt was an outstanding success, but also an alarming one. Thousands of listeners came into the city and packed Castlereagh Street, trying to catch a glimpse of actor Roddy Holmes, a midget dressed as a baby leering from a pram while Mitchell tried to push it through the crowd. The crush of people between Martin Place and Market Street was so great that people fainted, shop windows were in danger of being broken and police were unable to disperse the crowd for more than an hour.

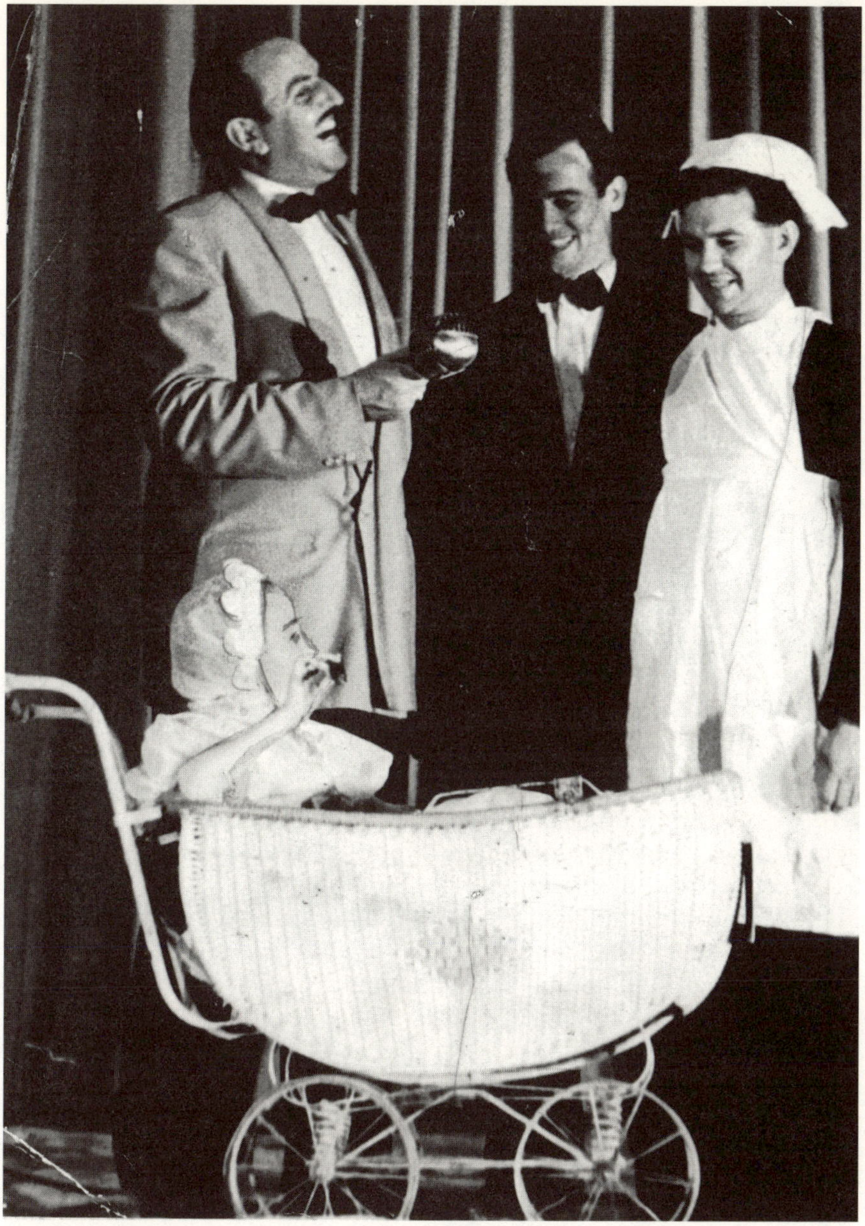

Bob Dyer setting up the 'impromptu' pram-pushing stunt on stage at the 2UW auditorium, Sydney. Roddy Holmes is in the pram with 'nursemaid' Ray Mitchell on the right and the author in the middle

When it was over Bob was charged with causing a public disturbance, went to court (with cameras clicking) and the magistrate gave him the edge of his tongue for his irresponsibility. He was fined £2 and in the process won himself thousands of pounds worth of priceless publicity.

After some months of living with Bob and Dolly I was able to rent

After a 'Can You Take It?' charity show at Sydney Town Hall, 1948. The author with Dolly Dyer and her mother, Mrs Mac

a flat nearby and my wife and son came over from Melbourne. But there was no forty-hour week with 'Can You Take It?'. I was on call day and night and weekends, according to Bob's whims, the demands of the program and other writing chores.

Then some turbulence in his career. The sponsor didn't renew his contract. At about the same time, the agency handling the account phoned me—at Bob's place—and said they would like to renew mine, have me write for somebody else and increase my salary by 25 per cent!

I asked them to wait while I took up the matter with Bob whom I felt had an option on my services. He said, 'Forget them, pappy. Stick with me. I assure you as a friend that you'll do better with me in the next two years. You have my word on it.'

I believed him, said 'no' to the agency and within a short time Bob had found another sponsor for CYTI. About this time I noticed a subtle change in him. He was growing tougher in business, tended to 'use' people, first with flattery and wining and dining, then when they had served their purpose bidding them a brusque goodbye. The smile in his publicity pictures was the same but now it didn't seem to reach his eyes. He became less tolerant with difficult audiences, too.

One evening, during a live broadcast from the 2UW auditorium,

Publicity shot of Bob Dyer in the 1950s

a drunk sitting down front kept on interjecting. His first comment was one Bob had heard before and had grown to detest. As he ran on stage in his country gear with ukulele in hand he yelled, as usual, 'Howdy customers, howdy. I'm the last of the hillbillies!' and the drunk yelled back, 'Can we depend on that?'

I saw Bob's neck redden and he grew angrier as the drunk continued to interrupt his jokes. When it was time for the first commercial—a recorded one—Bob dashed down offstage into the stalls, grabbed the drunk by the collar and had to be restrained by shocked members of the audience. He just had time to free himself and dash back on to the stage before the commercial finished and he faced the microphone again as his chuckling self.

Bob and 'Doll' were a remarkable combination; they worked together like a well-oiled machine. When Bob needed a typist, Dolly went to college and learned how to type; if screams were required in comedy sketches, Dolly did them (she was about the best screamer in the business); she organised publicity, learned how to use a camera, was a business partner as well as a wife and even a hard-working deckhand on Bob's yacht. (I can still hear Bob's voice echoing across the Harbour: 'Haul on that line, D-o-l-l-l!'). Together they wooed sponsors, befriended sponsors' wives as long as was necessary and nothing was allowed to stand in the way of Bob's continued climb to the top. He wore conservative suits more and more, hung up his ukulele and mouth organ, put away his hillbilly gear and 'yaller' boots and altogether seemed to want to put his days as a comic in vaudeville behind him.

By now, Dyer had only one serious rival: Jack Davey who during the war and since had kept pace with him in developing his talents in radio. Thanks to his rapier-like wit and ability to raise a laugh in his variety and quiz shows, Davey was running neck and neck with Dyer in a race for the title of most popular radio entertainer in Australia.

One Friday evening, after working all day with Bob, I opened the front door of my flat in Mosman and was surprised to find a heap of reference books, some files and recordings and a housecoat in a heap on the doormat. I recognised them at once; they were mine and only a few hours before had been at Bob and Dolly's place. Somebody had dumped them there without ringing the bell.

The penny dropped. Next day I phoned Bob and asked what we would be working on 'next week'.

His reply (still well-remembered) was, 'I won't be needing you any more.'

'What! How about our verbal contract—' I began.

'I can't talk now,' he snapped. 'I got guests' and hung up.

I never spoke to Bob or Dolly again and never found out why they did it.

Soon afterwards while working freelance with the ABC, I was told that Jack Davey was sorely in need of a comedy writer to help out with some new shows. Then—as now—gag writers were as rare as hen's teeth so I phoned and met him one morning during rehearsals in the 2GB auditorium in Phillip Street. I was surprised to find that the best voice and quickest wit in Australia was a shortish, roly-poly, middle-aged man with thinning white hair and an easy-going manner. We had a fruitful discussion, as politicians say and I accepted a contract (a written one, this time) from 2GB Macquarie Broadcasting to write and work with Jack. Apart from a ten-month stint in London writing for Tony Hancock and Stanley Black's orchestra with another Australian, Ralph Peterson, I worked with Jack, writing and acting in his shows for the next eight or nine years.

The first show I devised, known initially as 'The Club Show' was a gag-situation half-hour featuring Jack, George Foster and myself as an old character, 'Grandpa', who had 'a Sunday morning expression

Jack Davey

and a Saturday night mind'. It won top ratings for some years. Foster, humorist Alexander McDonald and I wrote it sometimes, but more often than not, Jack Davey and I wrote it overnight. His schedule, with four or five recorded shows a week was so crowded, there was no other time available to do it.

Looking back it seems incredible that we were able to think up original comedy material (which is written, not by the page but the line) in the small hours of the morning after we had both worked hard the day before. We would start at 10 pm (after appearing in a show in the auditorium) and complete the script by dawn. Rehearsal for the show commenced at 9 am and by 2 pm it would be recorded and 'in the can'. Then I'd go home by cab, usually falling asleep on the way.

Not Davey. He had business interests in a laundrette, a used car auction (he was often the auctioneer) and a restaurant. Also, he recorded the commentary for a weekly newsreel and these activities demanded much of his time.

Writing together overnight in a silent city building I got to know Jack pretty well and a human drama enacted in his office in the early hours one morning showed a side of him I had not seen before.

It was about 2 am when a grey haired woman wandered in. It was obvious that she had been drinking. We were surprised to see her; as far as we knew the only other person in the building was Monte, 2GB Macquarie's nightwatchman.

'Could you lend me a cup, Mr Davey?' she slurred. 'I want to make some coffee.'

Davey was impatient. 'I don't know who you are,' he said, 'and we're very busy. Would you leave us alone?'

'All I want is a cup,' the woman complained, and added in a hurt tone, 'I haven't got cancer you know.'

Davey sighed, handed her a clean cup from a trolley nearby and she staggered off. We resumed our writing. Soon after, Monte came in, rather worried. 'Was a woman in here just now?' Davey nodded.

'I'm sorry,' Monte said, 'but she's on the staff and it's a sad case. She's dying of cancer and she often stays on after the others have gone, drinks and does a bit of work to take her mind off it. Says she can't sleep at night. I didn't tell anybody . . . didn't think it mattered, see—'

'It's all right,' Davey said. 'Don't worry about it,' and Monte left.

The woman came back half an hour later and returned the cup. She was about to leave but Jack persuaded her to sit down and he talked to her in the most comforting way for half an hour. I was touched.

An even more bizarre happening a month or two later. Alexander McDonald (who didn't like late hours) had been persuaded to join us on our all-night writing chore and at about 1 am Jack got a frenzied phone call from his wife Diana whom he had left at home, alone. She told Jack that a man had forced his way into the flat, had a gun and wanted to meet Davey, who he said had 'seduced his wife on the radio' and he was determined 'to deal with him'.

McDonald and I had had a lot to do with scripted drama during our writing careers but this was the real thing and we were shocked, especially since we could hear every word Diana was screaming down the phone. But Davey didn't panic. He soothed Diana, warned her not to try anything stupid and added, 'Tell the man to come in here. I'll handle him.'

Alex and I were surprised and impressed. Was he being brave we wondered or simply confident that his gift of the gab that worked so well on radio would be equally effective with a gun-toting ratbag?

Half an hour later Monte, who had been warned, rang through and said he was sending a man up to see Jack.

Alex and I moved to the outer office and presently a gaunt, wild-eyed character in a raincoat appeared, his right hand in his pocket. He looked hard at us and as one we pointed to Jack's office. He went in, closing the door behind him.

For the next twenty minutes all we could hear were the muffled tones of the best-known voice in Australia rising and falling and very little from the visitor. We waited with thumping hearts for the sound of a fatal shot. None came. Then the door opened, the man in the raincoat reappeared and without a glance at us walked out. His right hand was still in his pocket.

We rejoined Jack but if we expected him to tell us what he had said to the would-be assassin we were disappointed; he made no comment. We got back to work and never found out whether the man had a gun or not.

There was plenty of variety in working with a top performer like Davey and a comparison here between he and Bob Dyer will serve to emphasise the differences between them.

Davey, although a self-publicist was a bland kind of man and behind his public facade a modest one. He thought little about his talent, and his one-in-a-million voice and razor-sharp ad libs made him the complete broadcaster. He thought laterally, was highly creative and original ideas kept on coming.

Bob Dyer, on the other hand wasn't creative at all, was not a writer but a 'switcher', took comedy ideas from many sources and adapted them to his needs. He kept in close touch socially with his sponsors.

Jack Davey didn't have to chase sponsors; they chased him and perhaps it is right to say that his only failure was his success; with so much talent it had come easily and didn't require much discipline. He had no requirement to 'do better' simply because, without much effort he was 'doing best' most of the time.

Dyer was an astute businessman, but Davey only *thought* he was. Although Jack made a lot of money he was addicted to gambling, and most of it disappeared as quickly as it came. In the early hours one morning, he grew restless and said, 'My spondylitis is killing me. I think I'll take a little walk around the block.'

From past experience, I knew what the 'little walk' meant and wasn't surprised when he returned an hour later and admitted that he had dropped £800 in a two-up game.

His gambling confounded his employers. 2GB Macquarie bought an expensive car for Jack's personal use. One day, the general manager called him in and said, 'Jack, I haven't seen the car lately. Where is it?'

'Oh, that?' said Jack. 'I sold it.'

'Sold it!' The manager was horrified. 'It wasn't yours to sell. It belonged to the company!'

Jack wasn't concerned and said no more about it until a few weeks later when he walked into the manager's office again, his pockets bulging with cash. He counted out a large part of it and put it on the manager's desk.

'Had a win at gambling,' he grinned. 'That's about the value of the car.'

It never would have happened with Dyer. Rumour had it that he still had the first dollar he ever earned. As one wag put it, 'The fivers slip through Bob's fingers like flypaper.' However, he was known to be unstinting in his generosity to his friends. And while Dyer was an outgoing professional on the air he was a very private man at home.

Davey wasn't so particular . . . he would talk to anybody and he enjoyed practical jokes. His best concerned the Archibald Fountain, that rather sombre centrepiece of Sydney's Hyde Park. It featured several bronze statues rising out of the water, one of which was a particularly muscular naked man wrestling with a bull. As a gesture to modesty perhaps, nature had long since coated it all over with a thick, dark green coating of verdigris.

One morning, to everybody's surprise, Jack came into the office at 2GB around 9 am. He was in a very good mood and revealed that in the early hours of the morning when nobody was around, he had waded into the pool, and using a bit of emery paper had polished up the genitals of the muscular man to a high brassy shine.

He led a contingent of voyeurs to Hyde Park to view his handiwork, but already a hessian barrier had been placed around it and inside, a man in overalls was applying acid to the offending area hoping to restore it to its former anonymity.

Dyer and Davey both had game-fishing boats, both went after the big ones and both were extremely sensitive about their public images.

When Jack was arrested in an illegal baccarat joint and had his fingerprints taken, he agonised over what the public would think. 'They will love you for it,' I told him, and as it happened I was right.

When Bob knocked a boy off his bike while driving home one night he was extremely worried. The child wasn't hurt but Bob bought him a new bike and went round and made peace with the parents, although I suspected he was more concerned about his public image than the boy's welfare. And when there were letters in the papers, deploring the wastage of good eggs and flour in the meringue pies Bob threw at contestants, when people around the world were said to be starving, Bob went to great pains to reassure the public that all the ingredients in the pies were of substandard quality and not fit for human consumption. It was not true.

In the 1950s, a 'feud' was organised between two great American radio comics, Jack Benny and Fred Allen. They traded insults and the campaign attracted a lot of publicity. With Jack and Bob in mind

Bob Dyer and Jack Davey. Good friends?

the same thing was started here, painting them as 'friendly enemies'. They had a publicity picture taken with them hugging each other and their hands in each other's pockets and they were smiling.

Actually, there wasn't much love lost between them. Davey didn't like Dyer much, indeed wasn't interested in him as a friend or even an acquaintance and he certainly didn't trust him, which wasn't surprising. On one occasion they made a pact for their mutual convenience, that neither would appear in a time slot already occupied by the other on a different station. Much was made of this 'friendly' agreement in the press, but it wasn't long before Bob broke it.

Then, towards the mid 1950s a chill wind blew through the radio industry. Television was just around the corner and it was known that it could make or break established entertainers. Australia's two top-liners reacted to it in different ways. Davey, relaxed, decided to wait and see, but Dyer, who realised that his outrageous 'Can You Take It?' stunts were a natural for television, took Dolly to America and the pair studied the medium for some months. When they returned, Bob had thinned down to a more acceptable silhouette and was sporting a shiny new hairpiece. He was ready.

Then an irreversible disaster for Davey, one which made his anticipated transfer to the new medium of little importance. A medical examination revealed that he was suffering from inoperable cancer. He made a few appearances when TV was launched in Australia but his drastic loss of weight told its own story. He was a dying man.

Bob Dyer however, made the transition effortlessly and 'Can You Take It?' was an immediate success on television, but not for long. The novelty wore off and wily Bob realised that stooges dunked in tanks of water and the rest with his cries of 'Aren't they good sports, customers?' was now old hat, so he pinned his future on the 'Pick a Box' quiz, instead.

It was a runaway success and soon his sleek image and jocular smile were a familiar sight everywhere. He won many new friends, including three prime ministers. He also won himself an OBE, and Dolly, whose main contribution on stage was bringing out contestants and introducing them to Bob was awarded an MBE by a grateful government.

Meanwhile, Jack Davey, now in decline continued to record his radio shows and one afternoon in 1959, I visited him at his flat and interviewed him for the ABC. We both knew it was near the end and our goodbyes, with talk about 'more shows' were an embarrassing sham. A few days later he was admitted to hospital and died.

Somebody at 2GB whispered to me, 'It's the end of an era' but it wasn't . . . not quite. His former rival, Bob Dyer was still going strong, his friendly image intact and with Dolly's tireless help keeping tight control on his money-spinner, 'Pick a Box'. It became the longest-running TV quiz program in the world.

Then, a bombshell! In 1971, when it had been on air for seventeen years, Dyer quit!

It was a shock for viewers and sponsors alike, but his timing made sense. Unlike Davey who died broke, he was going out well cashed up and as he explained to Percy Campbell, then general manager of 2GB, 'I want to get out while I'm on top, not later on my way down.'

He and Dolly sold up in Sydney, went north, caught many big fish and won many trophies, but finally retreated more and more from public gaze until they lived almost in seclusion.

In the late 1970s, Bob's health deteriorated physically and mentally, and he died at Surfers Paradise in January 1984 aged seventy-four.

A final comparison between the masters of quiz and the quick quip: when Jack died in 1958 his funeral was the biggest Sydney had seen . . . thousands of mourners he had never met lined the streets and many cried as the cortege passed.

When Bob died sixteen years later, Sydney's *Daily Mirror* reported that only five people attended the funeral . . . Dolly and four others. One of them was a chartered accountant.

The Great Depression

In today's society when rat catchers are called rodent eradicators, dentists' nurses are called oral hygienists and shoplifting is known in the trade as 'shrinkage', it's hard to believe that once old people were known simply as 'old people'. In fact, a society acting on their behalf back in the 1950s was called 'The Old People's Welfare Council' and nobody seemed to mind. Its general secretary was Mrs Jean Moffatt, a well-educated and elderly Scot who came out to Australia in 1928 as a social worker and after some years of depression in Scotland her first impression of this country was a pleasing one, but within two years Australia was in the depths of the Great Depression. When Mrs Moffatt talks about that disastrous period in our history, today's Australians may be excused for a feeling of deja vu. She recalls:

'In 1928 I was impressed by the happy-go-lucky attitude of the man on the street. Then came the Depression. It struck Melbourne before Sydney, at a time when I was doing charity work for the YWCA. People who had had regular wages for all of their working lives, who were paying off their homes, and luxuries like radios and suites of furniture and were heavily mortgaged suddenly found themselves in a position where they hardly had enough left over after the payments to buy food and clothing.

Coming from Scotland I had been taught never to buy anything except for cash. I had never engaged in hire purchase and when the effects of the Depression hit the people of Melbourne I realised that that was the way of life here . . . people were not thriftless. Simply, heavy mortgages were considered to be normal in Australia.

When the sackings began and wages stopped, furniture, even houses were repossessed and a moratorium had to be declared. In any case, the firms which had repossessed furniture didn't know what to do with it, they had repossessed so much.

While firms could not repossess personal goods, the awful thing was that it was not just a few people in this sorry state, but thousands, good, thrifty, well-meaning people who thought they were building for the future, then found themselves with nothing.

Young men were the first to lose their jobs and if they lived at home with their families they could not get sustenance (unemployment relief) Many went off to live in tent cities . . . "Happy Valleys" they called them and soon men, both married and unmarried were building humpies in "Happy Valleys" here and there.

I worked in New South Wales on the coalfields for a time and such settlements became quite permanent after a while with gardens all around. I knew of whole families who were reared in humpies while parents were penniless. No errant money came in, all they got was the meagre government handout husbands got for helping to build roads, stormwater drains and so on.

As the Depression worsened public confidence in the economy evaporated and small businesses as well as big businesses went to the wall . . . nobody was buying anything and finally, charities had little to give away. Men went rabbiting and fishing for food.

Before and in the early days of the Depression there was a government service for overseas workers who wanted to migrate to Australia. Many women from all walks of life came out under contract as domestics for only a few pounds, but with jobs scarce during the Depression, those already here demonstrated against newcomers when they arrived. Indeed, before long the YWCA had to set aside facilities to house the women who were practically destitute.

You would imagine that with so few jobs available and so much competition for work that people would be vicious with each other, but I never felt that. It was a real get-together of the people with everybody trying to help everybody else.'

These sentiments are echoed by Ray Mitchell. As a child in the 1930s, he remembers a poignant incident which illustrates how the desperate conditions of the time affected many Australians.

'My mother, father and I lived in a house on Henry's Hill at Gosford during the Depression. The rent was one guinea (£2.10) a week but we couldn't pay it for years. Dad drove a steamroller for the local council from time to time, was also a musician and sometimes repaired watches. Somehow we were able to make ends meet.

It was a common thing then for tramps to pass the house in their search for work. Not many were deadbeats. Most were decent men down on their luck and sometimes, half-starved, they asked Mum for something to eat, and because she couldn't bear to see anybody go hungry she always tried to oblige in some way. Sometimes she let them sleep on our verandah overnight.

One day a man stopped by and asked the usual, "Have you got anything to eat, Missus?"

Mum looked at him, realised he was a decent kind of man and was hungry and said, "I'll make you a sandwich." When she gave it to him he asked if he could eat it in our paddock at the back of the house.

"Of course," she said.

Soon afterwards my dad who had been sharpening a saw out there came into the kitchen and asked Mum if she had anything else she could give the man.

"Well, the bread's all gone," she said. "I suppose I could give him some soup. Has he eaten the sandwich already?"

"Not all of it," Dad said. "He gave half to his dog."'

It takes more than mere rhetoric to plumb the depths of the Great Depression, but Ray Mitchell came close to it. So does Mrs Lillian Paton, now ninety years old. She was a country housewife in New South Wales and remembers the speed with which the Depression engulfed everything.

'By 1931 we were hurting badly. There was a drought on to make matters worse, and the sheep were too poor to even kill for meat. Credit stopped and the banks closed. Nobody went hungry but there were no extras. I always made sure there was a saucepan of wheat on the stove. We boiled it up for porridge or if it cooked longer it could be turned out into a mould and eaten with golden syrup . . . we used it to thicken soup we made with kangaroo tails, too.

I had five sons and when their shoes wore out there were no more so one of them made sandals from bits of old car tyres and my sister sent us wornout socks which I cut down and joined for the boys.

We had no new clothes for years. Luckily both my sisters' husbands worked on the railways and they passed on their old uniforms to us. I used them with other bits and pieces to make clothes for the children. I also made my own clothes and my husband's shirts and pyjamas.

We blessed Mr Lang, the premier of New South Wales when he brought in child endowment for children under sixteen. At five shillings a week it meant an extra 25 shillings a week for us. As farmers we were allowed groceries to the value of 25 shillings a week also and unmarried men got about six shillings.'

Bob Paton, aged nine in 1930 lived at Merriwagga, New South Wales. He remembers the most important day of the week, Saturday, when everybody went to town to shop or to hang around.

The face of poverty, 1931

'There was a big hall in the town, and a number of cars were always parked behind it, well away from the main street. I asked my father why, and he said, "They haven't got enough money to pay for their registration and Sergeant Dwyer has told them to keep them out of sight, otherwise he will have to charge them."

One Saturday I was amazed to see Mr Swanston, a friend of ours wearing a pair of trousers made from wheat bags. Being an inquisitive nine year old I asked him why and Mum scolded me for doing so but

Mr Swanston said, "Laddie, my other pants were full of holes and I had to come to town today, so last night I made these," and he gave me a penny to spend on an ice-cream.

Buying new tyres for cars was out of the question for many people then. Like our neighbours. When the tyres on their car wore right down to the canvas, they got other old tyres, cut the beaded edges off and put the cases over them. Then when the tubes wore out they packed rolled-up wheat bags inside each and drove slowly into town and back at about fifteen miles an hour. It was ten miles each way.'

Life in the cities was even tougher than in the country. With jobs and homes lost, families became virtual nomads and with no roof over their heads humpies were the only solution. Soon communities of them dotted the landscape around Australian cities.

One of them, in Sydney, called' Happy Valley', built on vacant land covered a patch two miles long. Four hundred men, women and children lived there under impoverished conditions.

A child of the time, now an elderly woman says:

'There were eight in our family: Mum, Dad and us six children. Like lots of other men, Dad scrounged around in the tips looking for stuff to build our place with. He got a wooden frame together first and some sheets of tin for the roof and we all moved in. Flour bags were used for the walls. We split them open, stitched them together and nailed them to the frame, then soaked them with a mixture of lime, fat and whitewash to make them waterproof and to keep the fleas away. There were millions of fleas!

Mum made the humpy as nice as she could, Dad put up shelves and she lined them with newspaper and cut fancy shapes in the edges. The floor was made from bits of packing cases. No windows . . . just covers we could open or shut to let the air in. We had tins all round to catch water when it rained, because there was only one tap in the camp. It was a real meeting place for everybody, the tap. There was an unemployment camp committee to help if there was any trouble, but they didn't have to bother much.

Us kids did our bit: made regular visits to a biscuit factory and got bags full of broken biscuits for a shilling each and sold horse manure around Rockdale for sixpence a bag. The Salvation Army was kind, they used to give us food tickets. I think we would have gone hungry sometimes but for them. Lots of hawkers used to come to the camp and they sold just about everything: camphor, darning wool, soap, stockings, rabbits, fish.

We lived at "Happy Valley" for many years, because things didn't get any better and Dad couldn't find work. The camp finally closed down in 1939.'

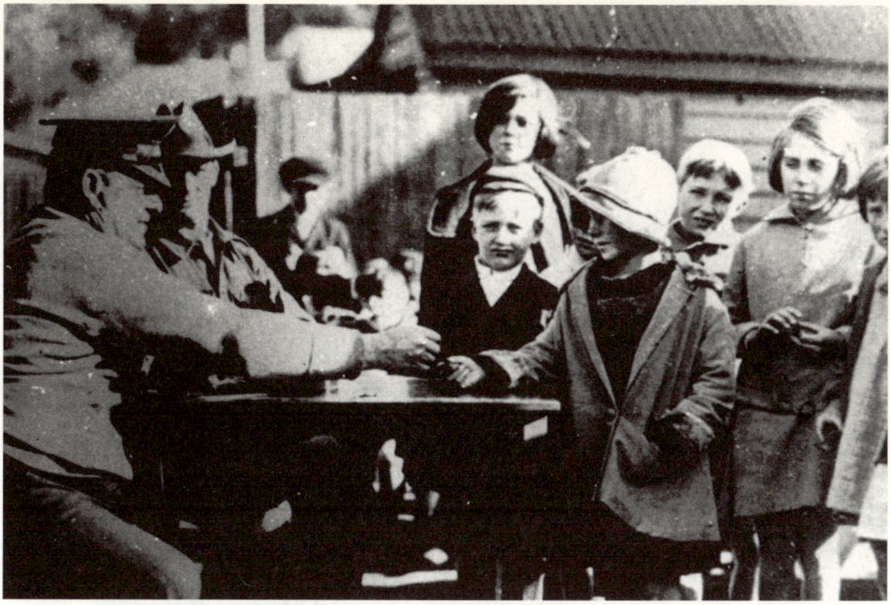

Children receiving food tickets from the Salvation Army

There were a number of makeshift humpy towns around Newcastle too, in the threadbare 1930s. One, called 'Hollywood' was sixteen kilometres from town and is now the suburb of Jesmond. Another child of the Depression remembers:

'I was practically brought up at Hollywood. Dad built our place from all kinds of junk. I remember that four-gallon kerosene tins were handy then and used for all kinds of things. Cut diagonally with a bit left at the back and spread into two halves they served as double sinks. We had one. Mum washed dishes and clothes in one side and rinsed them in the other. Cut and flattened out they were also good for walls or roofs. And a kero tin filled with water was always on our fuel stove ready for washing or for baths in our galvanised iron tub. Mum kept her flat irons on the stove too, ready for ironing. Not to mention a pot of soup . . . there was always one of those. During the winter months we sat on the floor around the stove for warmth. It was the hub of our home.'

Another elderly woman who spent her childhood in Hollywood recalls:

'Women had wooden boxes padded with straw and used them to save firewood; put half-cooked food in them and they finished cooking by themselves. Mum and Dad were so poor they couldn't afford to waste anything. Calico flour bags were used to line trousers and jackets and

A Depression lunch queue and 'shoes worn until there was nothing left of them'

skirts, also for making bodices. Many a garment had "First Grade Flour" and the maker's name on it. Women made oblong and oval mats from hessian bags with strips of different-coloured material woven into them to brighten them up a bit. Us kids used to sit on one in front of the stove.

Life was hard for mothers then, but terrible for fathers. Mine went out day after day looking for work but never found any. Worst thing for him was having to go to a Salvation Army soup kitchen at lunchtime for something to eat. He hated having to do that.

When our shoes got wet, Mum always put them in the stove to dry and made sure the door was left open. Nobody could afford to lose a pair of shoes then no matter how misshapen they were. People wore their shoes until there was almost nothing left of them.

All of the humpies at Hollywood were spotless . . . many had little gardens around them but people living in their own homes didn't like the unemployment camps. Their kids used to yell, "Dirty camp kids!" at us when we were coming home from school . . . used to throw stones at us, too.'

A common sight in the threadbare 1930s

Even harder hit perhaps during the Depression were families in business, people who had known great prosperity, then almost overnight were wiped out and were as poor—if not poorer—than some of their employees. Enid Jephcott:

'My father, Edgar Gibbons was a successful builder until the Depression. We lived in Cremorne, New South Wales and I know we must have been well-off because we were the first people in the street to own a car, a telephone and a gramophone!

Then the crash came. Dad tried desperately to keep his employees together in the hope that business would pick up; he even employed his foreman to clean our house and wash the floors. But things got worse and finally we had to leave our house in Cremorne. We owned another place in St Leonards a few suburbs away which was occupied by people at a rent of nine shillings a week, but they hadn't paid for six months, so Dad evicted them and we moved in. It was about all we had left.

Dad was still trying to keep his workers together . . . even paid fifteen shillings a week to one of his plasterers so that he could keep up with his rent.

There was community singing and other free entertainment at concerts each Wednesday between noon and one o'clock. Nobody got paid, of course. There was also a community soup kitchen at St Cuthbert's church hall near our home. Soup was boiled up in big gas coppers at the back of the hall and my father helped out by collecting bones from the local butcher and vegetables from greengrocers. I helped too by doling out soup to men on sustenance (the dole) and was always given an enamel billyful to take home afterwards.

Dad finally went to Coffs Harbour, and got a job building banana sheds. He was away three months at a time. Later my brother Charles, who was ten went up to help him and attended a local school. It helped Mum . . . it meant one less mouth to feed.'

Joyce West, another child of the Depression says she was luckier than most: she was one of few children who had shoes to wear to school.

'All of my friends were barefooted. And the difference embarrassed me so much I used to take my shoes off before I got to school each morning and hide them in my schoolbag. My mother always wondered how I managed to get my socks so dirty!'

Postscript

So much for the passing parade of yesterday's Australians with their opinions, their hopes and fears, their successes and failures and the injustices of a simpler time when Australia was young. In the main their voices have been stilled, the country has moved on and a comparison between life then and now would be odious, yet that feeling of deja vu remains, especially with the experiences recorded on these final pages.

Does history repeat itself? No answers here, but there may be a clue—or perhaps one should call it an illustration—in an unimportant event which took place in Melbourne in the late 1920s.

At that time, Marchants, a leading soft-drink manufacturer showed rare initiative in having a short advertising film made for showing in Melbourne picture theatres.

It began with a Marchants lorry, laden with soft drinks and pulled by four horses, dashing out of the factory gates. It was followed by another, and another . . . the lorries and horses kept on coming, emphasising the size of the company's fleet and the demand for its products.

Unfortunately, all of the horses were chestnuts except one. It was pure white and when it was seen appearing at regular intervals it was apparent that Marchants had only a few horses and lorries and once they had galloped past the camera they circled the factory, re-entered and came out of the front gates a number of times. In short, everything came around again.

A bit like life, isn't it?

Index